Avoiding Burn-ups on Re-entry

Mission Critical Briefs for Returning Expats

Linda Fraser Jacobsen

ISBN: 1-4392-5263-7
ISBN-13: 9781439252635

This book is dedicated to the Luther family, who were listening carefully the first time around.

Introduction

This book is a long time coming. For many years, after living and working abroad, creating cross-cultural training and re-entry programs for thousands of expats and their employers, and being given numerous opportunities to listen, learn, and later speak about these experiences to audiences around the world, it is time to hold still and put some of the best thoughts on paper to share with others. Many employers, despite the research, still do not invest in outbound expatriate training programs designed to better prepare their employees and families for what is to come on a foreign assignment. Worse yet, even fewer corporations comprehend the losses they must absorb for choosing not to do so. By sending your best and brightest out on foreign assignment without any advance preparation, you risk significant losses in many ways. In some cases, the strong survive and cope, but at what cost personally and professionally? In other cases, family pressures, poor adaptation skills, and attitudes all may lead to an implosion at home that carries over into a failed assignment, which translates into millions of dollars for an employer to replace that employee or family with someone new. What a waste of time, talent, and money!

From my experience, pre-departure training is like a crucial insurance policy, if done well. The upfront cost of training and preparing an employee is far less than the cost of a failed assignment or the cost of replacing that angry, frustrated, and resentful employee coming back home early. The impact on workplace morale and trust is obvious and often incalculable. The impact on self-esteem and family relationships is often more costly and damaging long-term. In the end, though, it all affects performance on every level. And this also affects cost.

For companies and leaders who recognize the long-term return-on-investment (ROI) of educating valued employees and working to prepare families for upcoming experiences with culture shock and potential losses in productivity as they learn to adapt to living and working abroad, I congratulate you. You have the vision to comprehend the value-added ROI you will have in a better-prepared and supported employee. You have learned that a happy family means a more productive and better adjusted employee, one who does not bring family tensions to the workplace. You let families know they are crucial to the success of the entire process, by offering mission critical support with house-hunting, school searches and visits, and general assistance at the new destination. Bravo! Your investments will pay off, long term, and you know this. But are you getting full value on your often multi-million dollar investments? Probably not. Let's look at why that might be the case.

While many companies and organizations *do* invest in their most precious asset–their people–they may not be aware of a bleeding out of talent they could be averting through simple training programs targeted to address this issue. What corporate hemorrhage am I speaking of? **Expatriate *re-entry*, or coming back home from a foreign assignment.** It sounds easy, doesn't it? How hard can coming home to a familiar place be? If you have never been an expat or one who has come home, I can understand your attitude. But know this: there is a lot of learning that takes place on a foreign assignment or a military deployment. The resulting bumps and bruises of that learning curve have made an impression on both the employees and their families that affects their coming home again in ways you cannot easily assess or anticipate. If you are unprepared for this journey–and I am speaking to both employees and families as well as employers–losses of many kinds will be sustained. This book is about how to anticipate and avoid this scenario and create long-term success and a strong ROI for all parties.

As I mentioned earlier, some agencies and companies are proactive and already address outbound expat training and relocation support. But many of these same companies do not address the critical hump of re-entry. For some of my clients, it is simply not on their radar at this time. For others, it is a tough matter of having to make a financial choice of where limited funds are best invested in the process for both the employee and the company, and the decision made is that outbound preparation serves better, if one must choose. So this book is really about helping those agencies, employers, expats, and self-employed global sojourners who do not have ready access to a formal re-entry training program through their workplaces.

For company leaders who are asking themselves why bother about training of any nature during the expatriate process, I have a few simple cost-driven questions to pose:

• Over the past five years, how many of your expats have had to return early from their foreign assignments or deployment for reasons other than family emergencies in the home country?

• What was the cost (both direct and indirect) to bring these people home and replace them on foreign assignment?

• **Of the employees who successfully completed their foreign assignments, how many either quit your firm within eighteen to twenty-four months and went to a competitor, or stayed with the company, but pushed hard to be reassigned overseas again?**

It is this last question that prompted me to write this book. While the other two questions are also relevant, I have included them to represent the true cycle of expatriation that begins at the pre-departure phase and goes through the overseas living and working assignment to right through the re-entry process. I hope that any financially savvy employer who reads this is already taking aggressive action to stop the bleeding in his or her own organization.

For those of you who are either self-employed or not receiving company support for your expatriate process, this book should serve as a useful and empathetic tool to anticipate and prepare for re-entry for you, your family, and your colleagues and customers around the world. My hope is that you are better able to settle in again and find happiness and satisfaction upon re-entry—and have some idea of what to expect and what to do about it.

Your comments, experiences, and suggestions are always welcome via e-mail. Many thanks in advance for taking a look at an often overlooked but mission critical element in personal, corporate, military, and financial cycles.

Safe journeys and happy landings,
Linda Fraser Jacobsen, January 2010

TABLE OF CONTENTS

Facts which at first seem improbable will, even on scant explanation, drop the cloak which has hidden them and stand forth in naked and simple beauty.

Galileo Galilei, 1638

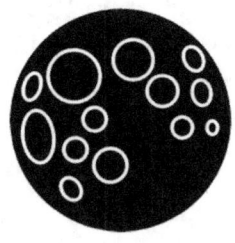

<u>Key Lessons Learned</u>

Judging by the number of résumés received over the years and the follow-up contacts made by former clients wanting something different once they are home again, there is a cycle on re-entry that few are paying attention to. Some companies or teams have noticed that if they hold some kind of quiet "welcome back" dinner for the returnee and partner with another manager and partner who have also returned earlier, they can defuse some of the tension by sharing stories or laughing over common experiences the home team simply cannot relate to. While this is thoughtful and useful, it is not accurately identifying what is going on or how to deal with it. A case in point would be how the returning military men and women cope with re-entry and the kinds of services being proactively provided. Who among us has not heard a story of a friend or relative who has served in war or worked abroad in difficult situations and has come home forever changed? The trauma is real, whether it is on a smaller or larger scale. It is what we do about it once we acknowledge it that matters.

So what exactly is going on with these returning global sojourners? Why are some of them so restless or frustrated? Why does it seem to be an issue getting them settled back into the patterns of their former teams and work environments? Why do some of them push for interdepartmental transfers within the first six months? Why do others simply up and leave as soon as possible on another foreign assignment with their families? And at the extreme end of the cycle, why do some choose to walk away from a very generous employment situation and jump to a competitor within less than twenty-four months of the return home? The answers lie within two areas: (1) ascertaining and meeting needs, and (2) realigning expectations.

Figuring out how someone is feeling after they return home is almost too late to intervene in the process. The time to address re-entry and all its resultant baggage is actually *before* departure. My company adheres to the practice of bringing up the re-entry process during outbound cross-cultural preparation programs. This way, an employer, employee, and family are all taking the cycle and its impact into consideration before ever leaving home on assignment. We identify where the challenges are most likely to come and we get ready to work through them.

If you have not had the benefit of outbound, preparatory training for a foreign assignment, there are many wonderful options to choose from. Programs that offer a more personal, family-centric approach, conducted in-person and before the house-hunting trip occurs overseas, is one. Books written by former expats on target locations, CDs, DVDs, and many other options abound. But few if any actually spend any time on the re-entry process, other than referring to a graph or chart depicting it as part of the expatriation cycle. At least there is mention of it, and this can build awareness in a savvy learner for the journey home again.

*Humans become human through intense learning,
not just of survival skills but of customs and social
mores, kinship, and social laws—that is, culture.*

Richard Leakey, 1994

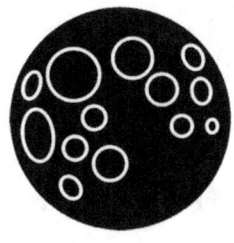

<u>Know Before You Go</u>

If someone had told you the trip overseas would be challenging and that you had a lot to learn going out, you'd believe this, right? So would your employer. So would your family. It only makes sense, doesn't it? You are going to a place you've never lived before, possibly a place where the culture differs sharply from your own, and where the language spoken and religions practiced and food eaten may be quite different from home. So we are agreed then. The expectation heading out is that life *will* be different and there *will* be adjustments to make in order to be successful.

What is not so readily apparent is that on returning home again, there will also be significant adjustments to make. Why is this? Let's look at the analogous theory of space travel and how time flows on earth versus far away from its gravity. According to Einstein's Theory of Relativity, things will progress at home pretty much at the pace they always have, but while you are a great distance away, much time will have passed on earth, more than perceived while you were away. Therein lie the difficulties. While you have been experiencing many new things while on a different trajectory overseas, your family, friends, and colleagues may have stayed on the same course you'd been headed on before you took off for parts unknown to them.

Think of the factors that are readily affected by making this move. Your behavior and decision-making abilities have been altered. Your family had to live differently and had to work together in different ways to learn how to be successful at this new life abroad, or had to learn to be successful without you at home with them. Your children were placed in foreign schools–some of them finer or more costly than ones they would have attended had you stayed home, possibly with language differences or at least differences in curriculum and instruction–and they have interacted with other peers not like those left behind in the move. Your partner or spouse may have had to give up a coveted position at work in order to accompany you on your assignment. The loss of self-esteem, income, and resulting adaptations that had to be made to live abroad with you were significant. You may have had to part with a beloved pet or separate from relatives who were elderly, ill, or otherwise needful of your presence and affection. You were all being pulled in many different directions and forced to adapt or fail.

You chose to take the assignment. You faced many new experiences, with or without preparation beforehand. Your partner or spouse did too. Your children and extended family did too. So what's the big deal?

You will never be the same because of the choice you made to go abroad.

This may sound melodramatic, but there is no reason for it to feel this way if we take a look at the process and how to anticipate what may occur, why, and what to do about it.

Nothing is so awesomely unfamiliar as the familiar that discloses itself at the end of a journey. Nothing shakes the heart so much as meeting—far, far away—what you last met at home.

Cynthia Ozick, 1989

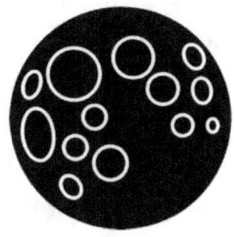

Time to Go Home Again

Most expats on assignment have a contract of sorts with their employer stating some kind of formal start and end dates for the assignment agreed upon. However, much experience has taught that these dates are not always firm or reliable. Think, then, of your expatriate assignment contract as a relatively firm calendar, but one subject to change (either shortened or lengthened) for a number of reasons.

One of the biggest reasons an assignment might be shortened is due to failure to succeed at the new location. Many times, if you ask the expats on group assignment how they are doing, and you take time to probe and listen a bit more deeply, you will find out there is a family struggling over there. Everyone knows which family it is, but is uncomfortable identifying the worker, for fear it could affect his or her employment status. These people have been through a lot together, and though they might not have known one another in the home country workplace, they will have bonded and share a common experience and will often tighten ranks to protect each other abroad. What have you done to encourage open and non-judgmental communication with your employees before they ever leave home, so they will freely approach you when help is needed for a struggling colleague or family? If asking for help is seen as admitting failure, you definitely have a policy or perception problem to address.

One of the biggest frustrations to key managers abroad is the feeling they are being "taken out" too soon. Some companies have arbitrary policies in place strictly limiting the number of years on foreign assignment. Why is this? When looking at this variable from the customer's perspective, the host country culture must be taken into consideration. A great example would be when a customer relations leader is asked to head back home after three years, and the customer from the host culture, typically a far more collectivistic one, is offended at this edict. After all, from their perspective, they are just getting to know this representative, and here the company is, whisking this person away just as they were beginning to matter. They quite naturally wonder if the company does not value them as customers? Does it think so little of them that it would take away their contact person, after they have invested much time in learning to communicate with, and trust, this person? Something to think about.

There are two reasons to raise this issue. First, the employer should carefully examine such human resource policies and eliminate any random rules such as time limits that might critically affect the bottom line in that office or region. Second, the family must consider that the host country clients might not wish for them to leave just yet, and they might need to plan on staying several more years to solidify strengthening relationships. For some families, this extension was never a consideration, and they automatically choose to return home again, since that was the original plan. For others, with effective ongoing communication while abroad, more flexible approaches may be taken. In general, though, when the home office calls you home again, you are not typically ready to pack up and head home. After all, *this* is home now, isn't it?

Breaking the news to your family may have widely varying results. At extremes, some jump for joy, others sigh with relief, but most are typically mixed responses. So many things to do before departure, places left to visit, people to inform and so forth, all may seem overwhelming, just as it did heading abroad. But these things are trivial compared to considering what your life will be when you head home again. Don't avoid thinking about it. Think further out in front. Talk with your family and begin realigning expectations, letting them know how life will start to come into focus once you head back home. By including the whole family in the experience, you are letting them know this is also a learn-as-you-go proposition for you too. No one will expect you to know everything or be in control of every detail, but they will trust that you are doing everything possible to respect and keep in mind their wishes and hopes as you are faced with choices and often very limited time frames in which to make decisions.

If you have left family behind by accepting a solo assignment or were deployed in military service, remember that life went on without you back home. You will have to make adjustments and not simply barge back in and start in where you left off. This is a great way to cause strife, even though you have the best intentions of demonstrating your love and your commitment and dedication to your family. Many families that have experienced these reunions recommend that the arriving partner remain a quieter observer for a few days, to learn what has been going on at home and what kinds of changes may have occurred.

For Expatriates Returning Home

What do you need to do to depart from your present residence? Many expats working for corporations have departure services pre-arranged as part of their benefits package. This type of service commonly consists of professional assistance with notifying your landlord that you are departing, as well as working to assure your security deposit is returned, utilities are turned off, movers and packers are booked and supervised, and so forth. If you don't have access to such a convenience, you will have to make plans yourself.

Make a list of things you need to do to exit your present life, and create a timeline for them. Start with the departure date and work backwards to the present. As you make your preparations, consider these issues:

• How will you ship goods home, or will you sell off items no longer needed? (Putting up a notice at work or sending out an e-mail list of things on offer is easy and quick.)

• Are you returning to a former residence that is being rented out? Do you have a renter to inform, and, if so, by when? If you are not returning there, have you begun the process to market that home and search for another?

• If you are moving to a new location in your home country, triangulate locations for school, child care and work, then explore living options based on how they feel to you.

• If you have school-age children with you, have you considered the time of year you are moving? Are you gathering up records and materials to bring home?

• What kind of job awaits you at home? Are there people you need to contact to explore all possibilities?

• Do you have a partner or spouse who has employment expectations in this location?

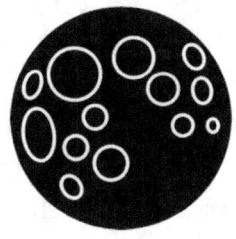

Bridging the Gaps

When you are living and working far from your home office, many elements change. Culture shock is expected when entering a new country, but many are equally shocked to find the office culture is also altered, even though the employer remains the same. You have mastered working in your home country work environment, and now must learn to be successful in another culture while trying to achieve your objectives. How you accomplish the simplest things can change when you are working in a different country and culture. The time you require to complete tasks, communicate across differences and time zones will all have an impact on your attitude and effectiveness. What kind of support system do you need in place to be most productive in your job? What communication links will you create and maintain to keep this information and action flow working smoothly for all concerned? How can you create successful systems and behaviors while abroad, and plan for your future once your assignment comes to an end? Better yet, how will you leverage this flow of information to prepare the way for your return to the home office, or wherever you are next transferred? Many people are so busy trying to figure out how to succeed in the new situation, they forget to consider the future as they are living and working in the present. Try to learn from past experiences while remaining open to new information and learning. Then take this amassed knowledge to build greater value for your employer or customer in the future.

If you are lucky, your company has built a smooth-running office that you will step into and learn on the run. On the other hand, you may find yourself having to rent space, furnish, decorate, and even obtain legal documents like licenses to operate in that new locale, all while trying to keep up with customer relationships in a foreign culture. But whatever the setting, it is still new to you, and you will have to come up to speed very rapidly to remain effective and valuable at your post.

Sometimes the intensity called for on location is so focused that it is easy to become lax about communicating with the home office team—until some crisis occurs and then you need immediate support and action. After all, by the time your work day is done, the time difference back home makes a call impractical, and hey, you are exhausted, right? If you have dropped the ball on staying in touch, why should anyone at home feel the urge to jump at your last-minute panic call? After all, you haven't bothered to keep them in the loop, so how can they be expected to care about a situation they haven't been apprised of? Making time to include people back home in what is going on at your location takes discipline and patience. Often you are the one who will stay late or come in early to make these contact calls, as you are in the minority and your time in the office may be more limited, if there are fewer support people at your location.

Instead of feeling resentment over having to be the one who always adapts to communicating across time zones, why not suggest taking a team approach to mission-critical briefings on a weekly or semi-monthly basis? Only you know what frequency of communication will work best, so try to negotiate for a schedule that suits you and your colleagues back home, so the team atmosphere can be built, maintained, or strengthened while you are abroad. With a regularly scheduled briefing, anyone can call in from anywhere and remain connected to the team and ready to react to any changes. If you make it short, consistent, tactful, concise, and add a dash of humor about life abroad, people will welcome your eventual crisis calls, which will come, with a more positive team spirit. They can catch a ball far more smoothly when they see it coming, right?

One gap element of working overseas that few deal with well is succession planning. Who is going to replace you when it is time to come back home? Are you sharing information in real time, to build a positive relationship with your host country customers and your eventual successor? Often our culture is so very competitive on an individual basis we compete to the detriment of our customers and our own budgets and timelines. Think about documenting the skills you have acquired, or the skills required most to be successful at your location. Sharing these insights might improve the selection process for your replacement when the time comes. Creating such reports gives you an opportunity to take personal and professional pride in capturing every detail of living and working in your situation and passing along the best lessons learned to whoever comes next. See yourself as a mentor and an expert informant. Capture and store information in ways your team can use for years to come. After all, your name will be on it and you will eventually get credit for having the vision to create, record, and maintain this data. You may also be positioning yourself to serve as an expert consultant on future projects linked to this nation, customer, or culture. You simply never know how well it will all work for you in the future.

If your partner or spouse has given up a successful career to accompany you or has decided to try to work from the remote location and this is a new experience for both the employer and your partner, this can create an enormous amount of stress as everyone figures out new routines, trust issues, time differences, work calendars, and so forth. In some cases, the employer decides it is not effective to work this way, and the job is withdrawn. What kind of network does your spouse or partner have in place in anticipation of this possibility? What are you doing to help your partner reach out and become linked in your new setting while remaining connected to the old one?

In some cases, your employer may provide job search assistance for your partner or spouse on re-entry, especially if they've given up a job to accompany you and suffered a loss of income for the duration of the assignment abroad. Have you asked? This service might also have been included in your original contract, and you have forgotten about the details over time. Thinking more broadly of your own career path, what types of internal communications may post job openings across your company? Have you looked, just in case there is something even more interesting than what your present manager has lined up for you once you come home? You may be able to negotiate an interview trip to explore the different internal job openings and meet the teams you might work with.

Typically, the re-entry worker has amassed some incredible new skills and may find it hard to fit in with the old team back home. Many do just this, and after a year of misery or depression, they force themselves to adapt to what was and plod on, looking down the calendar of years toward retirement. In a tough economy, fear might be a good reason to quiet down and conform, but it can't hurt to dig around and see if there are other positions opening up across the company that might make better use of your new skill assets. If you've been doing your homework and keeping great records of your experiences while abroad, you might have been sending out updates to key leaders and managers across other programs who might benefit from your talents. Ask around! In my experience, anything that is not classified can be forwarded out of interest. Your name may have more recognition value than you know—if you've made the effort to keep in touch and keep people in the loop.

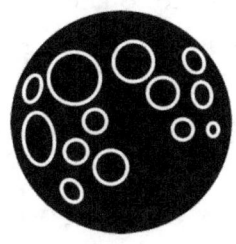

Contacts Back Home: Bridges & Gardens

Hopefully, before you ever left the home office, you were coached or mentored by a sharp former expat, who strongly encouraged you to build bridges and work hard to maintain them. What exactly does that mean? And why would you take time to do it?

If the present shifts in the global economy continue, there will be a constant barrage of corporate cuts and economic trends that call for a powerful network to remain gainfully employed or self-employed. The people you know, who know you best, are the ones who will always be willing to share your information with others, put in a good word for you, or even broker an introduction to key people in your working future. What are you doing now to ensure this outcome? Most people never do enough. They wait until they are unemployed, then ask for help, which, although it may be given, is not offered with the same confidence or enthusiasm it might have been had you taken time to keep in contact.

Building bridges means creating a detailed contact database and keeping those contacts warm, which is much like cultivating a garden. It takes time and discipline to do this, but it is one of the most valuable tools in your toolbox—and the most satisfying over a lifetime of friendships and personal growth. The term "networking" may seem cold, but if you look at the paradigm more as a garden, you will see the power of the reach of the image in your mind. Imagine a bumblebee in a perennial garden in bloom. The bee zips from flower to flower, gathering pollen. Think how the most admired and respected contacts and mentors appear to you in this image, perhaps as the tallest or most striking blooms in the garden. Who do they know? Where are they connected and how? Each link is a vital conduit to possibilities in your own future, if you sincerely appreciate and cultivate these friendships and opportunities and help them grow.

With our own clients, we often suggest a blog or website where the entire family can remain in contact without the hassle of sending unique communications to hundreds of contacts while abroad. In this way, many can share in the adventures and stories, but only one generic entry can cover most contacts. The more intimate family and friends' network might receive more personal communications, but the work is reduced and the time freed is better spent elsewhere. For employees trying to stay in touch back home, humorous anecdotes about life and work in the new location can be useful contact tools. You are teaching more than you know and paving the way for the wisdom acquired along the journey. A smart manager will see the subtle benefit your experience is bringing to the whole team. This is a terrific way to show your added value before you ever head home again.

If you work in customer relations—and who doesn't these days, on some level?—creating a detailed contacts database, one that your eventual replacement can add to or your home office team can access at any time, is a pearl beyond price! All the little things you have taken time to learn about your host culture colleagues, their families, their hobbies, gifts given, favorite foods and restaurants, and other valuable gems, can be stored and shared with your name and contact information attached to every communication or link. A great way to get credit for a job very well done, indeed, especially if you keep in touch upon re-entry and keep the database updated with your information.

Questions & Suggestions for Bridge Builders

• Who are the most influential people in your life? How have you kept in contact with them?

• What are you planning to do upon your return? Do you or your partner or spouse need some help getting the word out about job hunting or housing needs? These are great topics to share with mentors.

• Go back over some old, key communications records in your foreign office and fill in the gaps of missing information for your team or replacement. Create as clear and full a picture as possible for your team.

• Write templates of any processes or systems you developed during your time there and include your contact information for follow-up.

• Are you interested in entertaining offers from outside agencies? Does your family wish to remain in its present location, even if a change of employer is required?

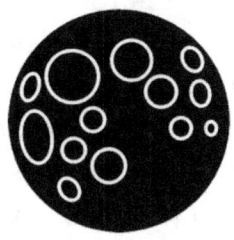

Expectation Realignment

Many things shift right under you when you move abroad. The same is true when you come back home again. Unfortunately, the most obvious differences cannot be seen, and therefore, they are often ignored by those who could most benefit from the knowing.

Remember when you first told people you were moving overseas? Do you recall the varying reactions? Everything from envy to sheer puzzlement. Everyone had their own inner picture of what you would encounter, though none had ever been there before. They were sure they knew what you would go through and, from their perspective, it either was or was not worth the effort to disassemble your life at home and head out for the unknown. It was your own sense of adventure, the challenge of the learning curve you would face, and the chance to live differently–certain it wouldn't be forever and, therefore, a more limited risk experience–that took you there. Sadly, many people who held negative inner pictures or saw your move abroad as something you would brag about are likely to still hold these views on your return. They may not reveal these opinions to your face, but their reactions and communications may indirectly demonstrate their beliefs. Change is hard for some.

Employers used to provide incredibly generous expatriate benefits. For many years there was a perception that moving overseas for the company meant maids, drivers, private schools, and a gorgeous place to live that you would never be able to afford back home. In a few cases today, this model still exists. For most, however, living in a local economy is not as plush or as profitable as one might imagine. In fact, some people actually lose money by taking an overseas assignment, depending on what the housing market was doing on departure and return, what mortgage lending rates are like, how tax laws affect your income and investments, and so forth. You may have chosen to spend time and money on world travel while living abroad, knowing this opportunity may never come again, nor might your health or situation ever be as perfect for it. This might mean you return home with less in the bank or the 401K than when you set out. Since not everyone has your priorities and opportunities, your choices are not readily understood. Sharing your options and reasoning with your friends and extended family, while abroad and upon your return, is helpful in the re-entry process. In fact, they may have valuable advice or suggestions for you to help minimize financial losses while living and working abroad, as well as when you transition home again.

If you know your re-entry landing position, you can start researching real estate, school districts, religious communities, and so forth well before it is actually time to come home. Try reverse-engineering your re-entry. Think about your arrival to the foreign destination. If you were fortunate to have assistance, you may have been given a packet of area information and maps and been taken on an area orientation tour with a local expert who had only your happiness in mind and not a commission. You were probably encouraged to explore first the traffic patterns from the office location and then work outward from there, looking at school options, housing, transit, conveniences, health needs, and so forth. You looked at areas and got a feel for them, to see if you could envision yourself living around there.

You can execute the same plan in reverse, too. If you know far enough in advance that you have a home leave trip coming up, you might take an extra day or two and stop in the future landing zone and buy some maps, take a look around, get to know a real estate agent or two, and establish a long-distance communication before it's time to begin searching in earnest for housing and schools and daycare. This way, you are able to set your expectations according to the real cost of housing, cars, furnishings, and other durable goods and services you will be purchasing on your return. You can keep abreast of market changes and cost variances on websites or by having local papers mailed to you for review. Often the same ads do not appear on-line that are in print. You also have these elements in mind before the actual re-entry transition, which you can share with your family, keeping them part of the process. You begin looking forward with real, accurate images of what can be, of what is possible.

Establish Priorities for Heading Home Again:

• Make a list of your greatest needs and rank them for importance. You and your partner or spouse may want to make separate lists and then come together to compare considerations.

• Relocating to a different city may mean you are able to buy less, or more, house than you are used to. Talking to local experts may help educate you on possibilities only they would know. Many expats wish they had known more about a place they were moving to so they could have chosen differently, in terms of housing, traffic, weather, and schools.

• If you have children figuring in the equation, think about sports, music, foreign language, and any other extra-curricular activities and convenience of access to them.

• Your housing needs may no longer be the same, either because you are transitioning to an empty nest, or soon will be, or perhaps you have learned to appreciate a different housing style. Talk it over with your family. Not everyone may agree on this one. Urban centers in one region of the world may be quite a different matter in another. Try to gently help young ones not to view things through rose-colored glasses.

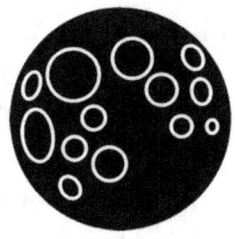

Self-talk

My mother is an amazing woman. When I was growing up and she was busy raising six children with my father, I would occasionally catch her muttering to herself as she faced off with yet another cheeky adolescent or angry toddler. Being ever-inquisitive, even as a very small, middle child, I would ask her why she was talking to herself. She'd laugh, hug me, and tell me that all the greatest people in the world talked to themselves.... She's never steered me wrong yet.

While everyone around you is full of sage advice on why you should or should not take a foreign assignment, isn't it funny how few of them have ever been in that actual situation themselves? Everybody has an opinion. Not everybody has a passport. The frank questions come at you from every direction. Then, once you do move overseas, settle in, adapt to the learning curve at full speed, hit a few bumps along the way as you keep learning, it's time to go home again. If you have a family living abroad with you, and the kids are old enough to say their piece, you are in for a confrontation–especially if they've made some wonderful new friends and have come to enjoy their new school and lifestyle, once they'd made up their minds to live with it. Your partner or spouse may be either delighted that the life abroad sentence is up, and he or she is free to plan a future in his or her own control again, or he or she may have created or found the dream career path of a lifetime and is not ready to have to re-think this through. And now you know what my mother was going through. You may not catch yourself muttering out loud, but you are going to have to think about how you are going to tell your family it's time to head home, or move again.

Start with your partner or spouse. Make sure the timing is right and the mood is calm enough to share this news. Do not fall into the trap of holding a family meeting where you drop the re-entry bomb on everyone at once. You are going to need an ally, especially if you have tweens or teens in the household. Talk to your partner and feel free to talk to yourself as you commute to-and-from home each day, as you work your way through the arguments, and try to anticipate what hurdles you will have to leap in order to move forward in a positive way. Think back to when you first came home with the news that you might be offered a job abroad. How did they handle it then? How have they changed as a result of their time with the learning curve in a new culture? Use every advantage gained by experience and begin researching the options, so your news doesn't become a free-for-all about where people want to move next. Since this is not realistic, it can be cruel to let them dream, even for a moment.

Most importantly, how *you* feel about all of this? Do you really want to head back to the office or team you were working with before you left, if this is the expectation? Are you facing a forced transfer of location in order to remain employed, but find you are not too thrilled about the offer? Are your key customers in your host country unwilling to let you go, and you feel like you are still in the middle of a great thing yet unfinished? Have you been operating in a fairly autonomous style and now will have to consider heading back to a team-centric or strongly micromanaged approach? Have your own new skills been inventoried, and do you know best how you would like to see them used? Have you had conversations with the managers and leaders who can offer jobs in settings that would make the most of who you are now? Or are you hoping to step back in time and pick up where you left off? How do you really feel when no one else is around?

Taking time to think these things through very deeply, before ever approaching your partner, is wise. You may discover truths that, until you faced this decision, you hadn't known were swirling around in there. So talk to yourself. What do you really want? What are your best options? What would make you happy? Be honest with yourself and then talk to your partner and try to put everyone's needs on the table. Not all of them will be met, but you can at least acknowledge the value of each family member's dreams, hopes, and goals, and work together to move ahead to the next chapter of your lives.

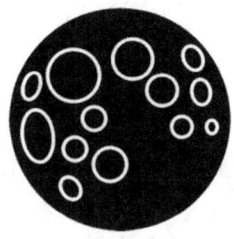

Values Shifts

If you studied the culture you were moving to when you took this foreign assignment, you probably studied values in some way. You may have even learned a little about your own values system and core values that are unchanging, no matter where you hang your hat. It's possible that even these core values were tested when in a cultural context so different from the one(s) in which you grew up or learned to become comfortable.

You may remember the first time you felt a conflict, when the home office or family or friends were tugging your choices and actions in one direction, but your new cultural circumstances were pulling you in quite another. There may have been situations with the home office, where you had to quietly step in and be a cultural interpreter, to smooth over a tense discussion that was getting out of control, because the other parties involved were unaware of the nature of the source of conflict. But you knew. You knew what was behind every comment, every gesture, every unspoken feeling in the room. In fact, sometimes you felt like you could read people so accurately, and alter your own reactions like a chameleon, that you wondered who you were anymore. This is a natural attribute of any global sojourner who is observant of what is going on around him or her and sharp enough to put it to use!

It's easy to become impatient with colleagues and friends who cannot so easily read the signals others may not even know they are sending. Over time, many expats find they have less in common with their homeland neighbors and colleagues, once they begin settling back in. Some expats notice these culture clashes or experience shocking little moments of impatience, even while they are still living abroad, but are popping back to the home office for meetings or communicating in teleconferences. You may have discovered you actually prefer some of the core values of the host country and culture, and you are no longer certain you want to go "home" again. Ignoring these issues will not make them go away. Hiding your feelings, when your core values collide with your more recently acquired ones, will not make life any more comfortable either. You need to decide that, if given the opportunity to live any way you choose, you wish to live under a certain set of core values. First, though, you must conduct an informal inventory of how your core values may have shifted, since you will have had to learn many new things in order to be successful abroad.

This is an exercise you might want to share with your family over dinner occasionally, especially when you know it might be time to head back home again.

Your colleagues, friends, and family, those who have not lived abroad for any significant time, will not understand why you are so impatient, withdrawn, angry, moody, or frustrated over being home again. They are still the same, so they expect you to be too. You are not the same person inside as you were when you left, but how can you explain this? How can you make them understand? (Hand them a copy of these essays and see if that helps!)

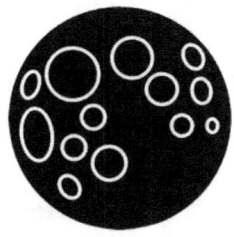

<u>Values Inventory</u>

Please answer the following questions. If you have a partner or spouse, answer these questions alone first and then come together and share your responses.

- Do you live to work or work to live? If given a choice, which one is really you?

- Do you prefer to talk, take walks, have long dinners with friends, or seek outside entertainment where you are more passively involved, such as film, theatre, etc.?

- If there are others around, are you more likely to stay quiet and keep peace rather than speak openly about what's bothering you?

- Do you have to solve every problem or can you let some things work themselves out?

• Are you most comfortable doing several tasks simultaneously or completing one task at a time?

• If you create a list, do you prefer doing the tasks listed in order or does it not matter?

• Do you take a long-term view in planning or are you more of a firefighter here and now as it unfolds?

• Are you annoyed if someone is on their mobile phone during your meeting or are you used to such interruptions and consider them natural and expected?

• Would you rather make a list and get it done or stop and have coffee with an old friend when you have that list in your hand?

• Are relationships almost always more important to you than achievements?

• Do you need a lot of space and closed doors in which to work well or can you share a space and focus even with lots going on around you, including interruptions?

• Will you circumvent a chain of command to get an answer or action or will you adhere to the structure?

• Do you believe that rules are made to be followed or may be broken depending upon circumstances?

• Would you rather work alone or with a team?

• Must everything be in its place or can you let things fall where they may?

These questions raise issues of personal and cultural values such as understanding your level of individualism, your need for harmony vs. control in dealing with life and work, your ability or comfort level with being single- vs. multi-focus when it comes to tasks and thinking, whether you tend to be more or less direct or indirect in your communications with others, and whether you work within or around a hierarchy or chain of command, and so forth. Most people find their responses are more of a relative pendulum swing along a spectrum, where the pendulum will land more one way or the other depending upon the culture, the nature of the interaction, and the depth to which you know and trust the other parties involved.

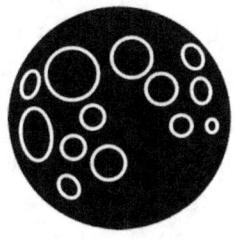

Workplace Dynamics

What was your home office setting like before you headed abroad? What was your role there, and what skills did you most utilize to be successful? If you think back to your last evaluation back home, what goals and skills were you praised for, and which ones did you need to work on the most? Do you recall why you were selected for a foreign assignment? How do you feel about where you may be returning at the home office?

Many expats tell me the hardest thing about coming home is heading back to an office dynamic that feels too constricting or confining. When we explore this, we see many times that the overseas workplace setting is far less crowded, and there is more room for cross-training and personal growth; however challenging or stressful the situation is at times. How does this translate to coming home again? Not well. You have acquired many new talents and skills because you had to, and now, back home, there is little or no call for many of the systems, processes, or strategies you created abroad, but they are still in your own skill set or inventory and waiting to be used again. The sad part is, no one is asking for them. No one knows you have them. If this sounds depressing, it is. This is one reason why highly talented people leave their workplaces and head for brighter shores after being home only a short time, the average time being about eighteen to twenty-four months.

A smart manager will start asking his or her people about the skills and talents they acquired while working abroad as part of a periodic debriefing cycle. A wise one will find ways to put these broad spectrum gifts to work for company profit and personal satisfaction even while still abroad! This simple strategy can help companies best use and retain their greatest talent long term.

If, however, you are unfortunate in your company's leadership, it is up to you to raise this conversation, report on your own assets, and suggest how they might be best used by the company. This is one of those key bridges for communication we talked about earlier. Take responsibility for communicating your own assets and how best they can be utilized for maximum ROI. After all, the company invested a lot to send you abroad to work for them, why not take advantage of what you gained as a result? Reach out to people who can influence decisions on where to place you when you return, and be sure to report to them as you settle in and adapt to the new workplace setting. Things change faster than ever now, and the best companies will adapt more quickly to respond to the changes or even lead the way in new markets. They need you, and they need what you know. Your job is to make sure they get that message.

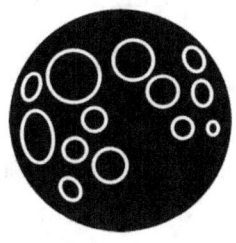

<u>Workplace Inventory:</u>
<u>At Home and Abroad</u>

Now think about where you are now. What is your role, and what skills are you calling on most to be successful? Make a list. Don't be modest!

• What are the differences between home culture and foreign culture business planning methods? And of these, at which do you excel?

• How is information organized and disseminated in both settings, and where are you strongest?

• In personnel issues, what were some key differences between home and foreign business practices?

• Leadership styles vary greatly from culture to culture and even within organizations. List the styles you work with best and which ones are suited to particular settings.

• How is argument or persuasion used, or not, in different cultural settings, and how adept are you at functioning in each?

• How were decisions made in both settings, then and now?

• Methods of evaluation and assessment vary greatly and are used for different reasons. What are the strongest similarities and differences you observed, and how would you put this knowledge to good use?

• How many of these skills were acquired on the job abroad?

• What took you the longest to learn, and what did you like most, and least, about what you had to learn?

This mass of questions is not designed to drive you crazy, but to help you quantify your skills and talents, then try to align them with your greatest sources of satisfaction while working.

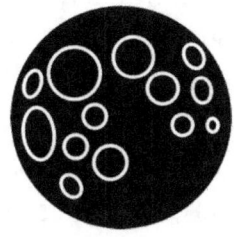

Autonomy No More

One of the hardest re-entry experiences is the one where you feel the reins tugging at you, just when you are ready to charge off in what you are sure is the right direction. Sound familiar? You feel like you are choking on rules. Rules that you have been away from and apart from for the duration of your foreign assignment. But everyone expects you to pick up right where you left off, as if you'd never left. You may not even recognize this for what it is and find yourself feeling furious and impatient at the end of a team meeting. You feel like slamming the door as you stomp off, sure that everyone in that room you just left is an idiot and cannot see what you are certain is coming.

The team back home may look at you as if you are crazy at times, especially when you speak your mind. They are wondering why you are so short, even arrogant, with everyone, and they are amazed at your views and at how freely you express them in public. The colleagues once closest to you pull back, worried they will be tarred with the same brush of outspokenness. If you try to express the reasoning behind your perspective, it often includes a phrase like, "When I lived in Dubai..." which shuts down the ears of the competitive colleagues around you, as they assume you are bragging about an experience they lack, as opposed to listening without judging and, eventually, learning from your experiences abroad.

You spent years learning about the host country and culture, how to build relationships and trust across vast chasms of difference. You were successful over time. You learned to trust your instincts, which were finely honed by having to learn constantly in a foreign environment. You learned to listen well and be an even better observer, so you could place nearly every communication in its proper cultural context. You became versatile, adaptive, and lightning-quick responsive. You had only yourself to depend on in most settings. There was no one else to confide in, compare notes with, or lean on. You were it. How insulting it feels to come home to people who feel like their opinions should influence your decisions! You are in control. You have been for years now. *Does any of this self-talk sound familiar?*

You may have become so used to making completely independent decisions in the foreign office that you find you have little patience for the consensus process or any team discussions back home anymore, let alone the time they take. Your exposure to a plethora of new ideas, ways of doing things, as well as cultural differences, communication practices, and other workplace elements, has changed your outlook forever. You have learned to lead by action, by better listening and observing, and have much to share with your team, if only you could get them to listen. Your greatest strength now probably lies in customer relationship development and how to make that customer one for life. The things you know now are of such great value, and often so critical in their timing, that you feel thwarted at every turn back in your old office setting. They just don't get it.

Now you know why taking the time to identify your workplace inventory of skills is so crucial. It is information that you can share on an ongoing and objective basis, which in turn will allow management to better place you at work upon your return to the home office or wherever they send you next. The sooner you begin articulating these skills and how they may be of use to an employer, the more likely you are to end up a happy statistic instead of a miserable one.

If you did not take time to fill in the answers to the Workplace Inventory in the last section, don't avoid it. Find time and get it done!

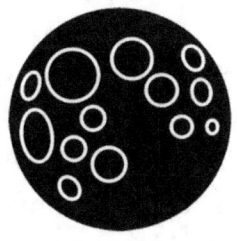

Global Skill Sets

When companies come looking for global talent, they are looking for people with very specific skills, usually acquired from living and working abroad. I call these strengths Global Skill Sets. We've alluded to several of them in the previous essays, but the key term over all these skills would be Adaptability. Here comes that chameleon again.

You have spent a lot of time learning, listening, observing, and even trying out new ways of thinking and communicating in order to keep your life moving forward in a different culture. It is difficult to identify each and every new skill acquisition, but it is possible to create concept groups that help to quantify the strengths you can now offer to other employers or bring to other leadership opportunities. This range of skills is going to be important to you, whether or not you make time to take an inventory. Why? Because your future happiness at work and in life may well depend on how much you have come to value using them and have a need to keep using many of them to find the greatest personal and professional satisfaction. So if you sit still long enough to create an inventory of additional skills obtained due to foreign assignment, you will have built a value-added proposition you can use for many purposes. The one that comes first to mind is your résumé.

Whether internally or externally circulated, your new skills should be documented and shared with key leaders who may spot opportunities best suited to your range of talents. By sending periodic updates and communiqués about your foreign assignment and the value you are bringing to the dynamic, the final touch will be to formally or informally document these skills, share them with key contacts, then follow up with each one to see what types of upcoming opportunities might be a great fit for you and them. From client discussions, taking a proactive approach on this front has often generated highly positive results, and, in many cases, multiple offers from which to choose.

If you are a manager or placement specialist reading this, hopefully there is action being taken to elicit this data on an ongoing basis from every expat manager or potential global manager in your database. Create your own matrices outlining the traits necessary to advance your team and start matching up your re-entry employees with more positions better suiting their new talents. Encourage home office leaders to understand these new skills and why they can impact the company's bottom line back home too. Helping everyone understand the power and knowledge wasted by not fully utilizing these people and their new skills is a real challenge. Usually the unimpressive retention rates tell their own sad story. To create your own inventory, start simply. Look back on your own cultural adaptation and the first lessons you learned and go from there.

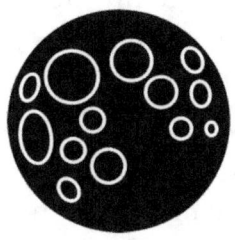

Global Skills Inventory

• What were the critical skills required for you to take the foreign assignment in the first place?

• Were there skills you knew you were strong in that made you confident in applying for a foreign assignment?

• What were some of your deficit areas, and what did you need to learn or change in order to be successful in the new cultural setting?

• After working abroad for significant time, would you say the skills you were most heavily relying on to be successful were the same ones the company had initially identified as key skills? If you can identify additional or different critical skills between company perception and your workplace reality, then do so.

• What skills did you need to master first, second, and so forth? How frequently do you use each skill now and under what circumstance?

• How often have you experienced a moment where you had a solution to contribute once you were back home again, and that information was gained as a direct result of your experiences abroad?

• Don't forget to list languages learned!

• If you have a chance to express your preferences in a new position back home, what skills would you most like to put to use?

• How can what you learned benefit your team, your customers, and your employer?

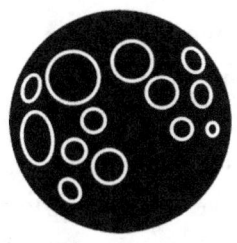

Re-establishing Life Patterns

When working with families before they go overseas, I always take time to warn them that often the re-entry bump will be harder and stronger than the one they expect to experience on the journey out there…. After all, when you leave, you know you are going somewhere different. You expect the language, the culture, the food, the transit systems, and even the way you choose to live with your family to vary greatly from your life at home. *Home.* This word connotes powerful images, but above all, it means we know what to expect because it is familiar and comfortable and known to us. Moving changes everything!

In choosing to move abroad, we discover that accomplishing what would have been the simplest tasks at home have become challenging, enigmatic, and horribly time-consuming. Think about how many ways you know how to get to-and-from the office right now. Whether you are at home or abroad, there was a time when you did not have all these options freely sorted in your memory, able to access at a moment's notice. Life abroad is full of such deeply embedded mental models--suddenly worthless in the new environment–and the expat and family have to scramble to define and build a new life with mostly new rules. This process is The Learning Curve.

Many expats have mastered so many new things, it is hard to talk about them, let alone identify and keep track of them. Others have a way of coping with the changes by trying to imitate as closely as possible what was left behind; patterns of daily life that brought comfort and familiarity in the unknown. Some people will go so far as to try to find as close a match as possible in housing or schools, for example, in the host country, so they can minimize their "culture shock." Others purposely seek differentness in the expatriate experience, intrigued by the opportunity to live differently, knowing it is not forever. Where on the spectrum do you fall? How patient or impatient are you with The Learning Curve? How patient or impatient are your accompanying family members?

The best advice heard over-and-over from re-entry families is to focus on the youngest family members first, get them settled in as well as possible, then work up to the needs of the remaining family members. While taking time to care for others first, often your own sense of being overwhelmed dissipates entirely. This advice makes sense. The younger members in a family often have fewer complications in their lives and fewer requirements for their happiness. The time to help them find new life patterns will be shorter than what may be required by older family members with more complications to discuss and deal with. This process should begin as soon as you know it's time to come home. If you are employed, ask your employer for a trip home to find housing before it's time to move the whole family back again. Having a house to move into and schools already selected before the kids get there will save headaches and stress, as the parents make the decisions without their children's "help."

In cases where older children have input on where to live, which school to attend, and other weighty decisions, there is a cautionary note to share. Many teens may at first feel empowered to be in on discussions of this magnitude, but what if they are later unhappy at home or school over time? Because these sensitive young adults feel that their input at the time of decision-making was perhaps to blame, many of them may not feel right later telling parents that they may have chosen poorly, so may remain silent and miserable. Many parents recommend listening to what their kids have to say, but letting them know the final decisions rest firmly with mom and dad.

For some families with older children, returning home may be full of small pitfalls. Differences in legal age for drinking alcohol, driving a car, smoking, and other freedoms may either be ruthlessly curtailed or suddenly available to teens. Clear limits and rules must be set at home, before something has the chance to get out of control. If your son or daughter was living in an area where he or she had a lot of relative luxury, status, popularity, and perhaps a lot more freedom in certain ways, you may have a rebel on your hands when you get home. It's hard on a teen's ego to drop into sudden obscurity and have to adjust to life without privileges that were commonplace overseas.

Returning to a former workplace is not as easy as you might think. Many colleagues assume you are the same person you were when you left. After all, you still look the same and sound the same, don't you? The patterns of living and working abroad became familiar and comfortable to you over time, and they will take equal time to unlearn. You may find you no longer enjoy or relate to certain office traditions, after having been exposed to other values and communications systems. The imagined tightness around your collar, from constantly having to wait for others to decide things you used to be able to do without consulting anybody while abroad, is grating on you. The skills you acquired abroad have no place in the old setting, and people don't seem open to listening to your stories or how you might now solve a problem.

Top off all this with a partner or spouse who has to hunt for another job again. Unless you are very fortunate, typically only one of you has a job to return to in your new location. Your partner or spouse may have had to leave a lucrative position to accompany you abroad, and that subsequent loss of income and self-reliance hurt you both. Now these issues, once eventually put to rest in the host country, come back out on the table. It is hard to be supportive of adjusting kids, moody or silent teens, and a spouse or partner who is struggling to be upbeat in a down economy, looking for a great job after a gap of unemployment. This is a good time to help your partner conduct his or her own assessment of skills gained through the move abroad. A cover letter explaining not only the reason for the gap in employ-ment, along with resulting personal growth, might be just the thing to get the phone ringing and the inter-views set up. This is also a great time to activate that garden full of mentors you've been cultivating. Those bumblebees go everywhere!

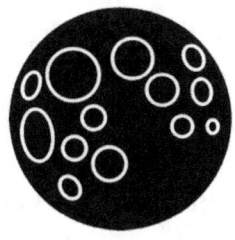

Latitude with Attitude

The pressure is coming at you from every direction. You thought you could just slip back into old routines, habits, friendships, without losing a beat. After all, this is your home country. You know how everything works without a learning curve. How hard can it be? Yeah, right. If you thought this, imagine how your children are feeling. Is anyone talking about the literal impact of re-entry at home or at work? Probably not. So, you need to give yourself and your loved ones room to breathe, to adjust to what should, logically, be easier to face than it was when you headed abroad, even though it doesn't feel that way many days.

Teachers in the classroom with your children have no idea what experiences they have encountered. Teachers see a native speaker, dressed and behaving pretty much like every other child in class. But your child may be bored in school, after performing at a more advanced grade level in certain subjects while abroad. Or, at the other end of things, your child may struggle with simple socialization, reading, or creative writing, if these growth opportunities were reduced or unavailable in the foreign setting. Make extra time to consult with school officials, and try hard, wherever possible, to put your child into a school at the beginning of the academic year instead of the middle. If you have a chance to designate when you move back home, do consider coming home over the late spring or early summer window so your family has some down time to adapt, get to know new friends or neighbors, and find some new routines that feel good once again. The best thing about this window in the U.S. is that most houses come on the market at this time of year, as many families try to complete a school year with children before changing districts on them.

Your partner or spouse is nervous about having to start over again. He or she has just spent the past few years learning to live differently. Now it is time to pull up stakes and head into the unknown again, at least on the job front. As you search for housing together, keep the economic conditions, the relative demand for the job being sought, and your budget in focus. Many families cause themselves undue stress by reaching for a home and mortgage that requires two solid incomes coming in every month.

What is wrong with setting your sights a bit more realistically? If only one of you is gainfully employed and job opportunities are looking rather limited, why not consider searching for a home based on one income? This sounds revolutionary to many who have bought into the "bigger is better" mythology, but much good can come from this.

Families who have a mortgage that can be paid each month on one income have so much less to worry about if something happens to one job or one partner's health. What if one of you is unhappy in the new location, but due to the financial pressure caused by the housing you chose, feels unable to share these feelings and find another job? This kind of stress often rolls right through everyone in the family, all without anyone knowing why everyone is shrieking at each other, and why the younger kids aren't sleeping so well. Some couples decide to rent a home the first year back, take their time looking at the schools, the commute to work, the traffic, the weather, conveniences, and the true cost of living in that community. Then, if both partners feel that the move is a sound one, they begin to search for a home they can afford, with jobs they are content in performing. Think about it. What's the rush? Check with a tax advisor, in case you have tax implications, time restrictions, or rollover deadlines to consider in making your decisions.

And what about you? Your workplace is the same. You may even park the same car in the same space after having been gone for several years. But you are not the same. In many ways, you have tested yourself, pushed yourself, and mastered a myriad of new skills that seem to have no place at the office back home. Give yourself time to talk these feelings through, perhaps with a trusted mentor who has also made a re-entry move, and see if you can settle in again. If not, keep your partner and family posted, so if you decide to make a move, they are supportive and prepared, instead of bludgeoned with it.

Your colleagues will be happy to have you back, unless your behaviors and communications at work somehow make them feel condescended to. Sometimes your overseas adaptations come out in the workplace back home, or you feel the need to talk about it. Others, some of whom may see your career as in competition with theirs, may perceive your stories, suggestions, or ideas as threatening and may try to cut you off. This can be very hurtful, but try to remember it hurts them too. They may be envious that you lived and worked abroad, while they either turned down the same opportunity or were not selected for it. Their problem can quickly become yours, if you don't adapt to the reality of the setting back home again. How you phrase things and how you share ideas may now require a bit more thinking and planning than simply opening your mouth and speaking. Gee, doesn't that sound a lot like what you had to do to adapt overseas in a foreign culture?

There are no conditions to which a man cannot become accustomed, especially if he sees that all those around him live in the same way.

Leo Tolstoy

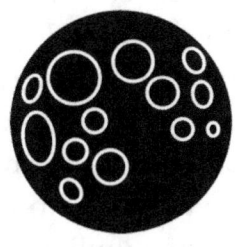

Mourning What Was

To talk about mourning what was, we have to look at many variations on the theme, to pay true attention to the process of re-entry. It can be perilous and painful to a few, but perhaps it doesn't have to be this way. If you had any preparation prior to your assignment abroad, you were taught about culture shock and the ways it might manifest in you and your family. Heading home again can also have a similar bump. For most, it is actually a bigger bump to come back to where you once were. It doesn't seem logical, does it? But then, not everything about human nature is controlled or contained with logic. Grief counselors know there is a process of mourning most people go through, whether they notice it in themselves or not. It is much the case with expats and families coming-and-going. Change if, in and of itself, a death of what once was. Everyone deals with change differently.

When you first moved abroad, unless you are very unusual, you missed certain elements of your former daily life and the things that made up a day, even if only for fleeting moments here and there. You may not have been homesick or really missed most of what was left behind, because you had so much to master in your new locale, but there are likely to have been moments of nostalgia, perhaps surrounding the stress of new routines, getting along in a new language, missing a favorite food or product from home, or whatever your family faced....

It took a few months–maybe, or for some, a year or more–to finally begin to view the new location as "home." In rare instances, where you have family members who cannot wait for the foreign assignment to come to an end, so they can resume their old lives, this feeling may never be outwardly identified or discussed, mostly to avoid confrontation with less well-adjusted family members. What is said about attitude being everything is not far off the mark, is it? So whether you want to be somewhere or not, learning occurs. Adaptations must be made, to a point, even for the most resistant or maladapted expat. For these people, mourning what was left behind begins the moment they leave home and get on the plane for the new job posting.

My sympathies to those of you who have run into and felt constantly punished by these people. It is brutal, dealing with the guilt they gleefully pile on you as you strive to do a great job, make the most of the opportunity, and try hard to put a good face on their misery. You eventually learned to let them wallow in it, because you had to keep your distance to save yourself. You were also not surprised when this miserable human being ended the assignment early, skulking back to the home office feeling embarrassed or ashamed, to avoid marital friction or worse. This costly outcome is one of the biggest pitfalls in not selecting or preparing people adequately for life abroad, and the impact it can have on not just the employee, but the entire family and the company's bottom line is very significant.

Coming "home" is fraught with sameness. Some people are overjoyed at not having to think through every element of a day anymore, now they've come back to life on auto-pilot. You can quickly find new routines, but you are lacking that enormous uphill struggle to master a new culture and everything that life abroad entailed--The Learning Curve. You miss those private, precious celebratory moments of saying, "Yeah! I got it right! I am getting the hang of this new situation. I can do this!" You may even feel your work is not nearly as challenging or as interesting as it was abroad. That's okay. You are not alone.

It took time for you to learn all those incredible things and even more time to come to appreciate or enjoy some aspects of life abroad. It's only natural you will miss some elements of what came to be part of your new daily life. Think about when you first arrived abroad and how overwhelmed you felt on occasion wondering if that feeling would ever subside. It did, didn't it, as you learned and found new ways to cope? Or maybe you went beyond mere coping and thrived on succeeding and finding happiness in that new life? So if you did find joy abroad, you can expect you will feel even more deflated at times about coming home again. That's okay too. And you are not alone in this experience either.

Finding contentment again may take time, much more time than you are willing to allow yourself. Try to think back to the things you seemed to miss the most about your life back home when you lived abroad and sort through these feelings, products, people, organizations, or whatever they were, and see how you feel about them now. Over time, you may be surprised to find that what once seemed absolutely essential to your happiness does not hold the same place as a priority in your life anymore.

All changes, even the most longed for, have their melancholy; for what we leave behind us is a part of ourselves; we must die to one life before we can enter into another!

Anatole France, 1881

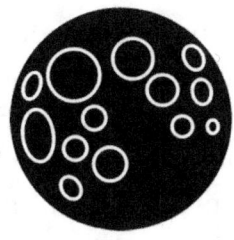

Hear Me Out!

Have you ever been in a meeting where a discussion turned toward a topic in which you have some significant experience and are about to explode if you can't talk about it right then? You are not alone. Almost every expat manager who served abroad in a real decision-making capacity gained some valuable skills on foreign assignment. The problem is, not everyone in your home office understands or recognizes this, for various reasons.

Many clients have shared experiences where they were shut out of conversations once home again, as if their time abroad somehow excluded them from full participation in meetings. Others have been literally shut down by abrupt comments, usually sparked by some illogical sense of competition, along the lines of, "Yeah, Fred, we know you were in Russia. You don't need to brag about it...." These barbed comments are part of the re-entry cycle that cause the most hurt and frustration in the workplace environment. At home, you might encounter similar comments when people ask about photos or some aspect of life abroad and a so-called friend pipes up with a comment like the one you just heard at the office. Many people will be thinking these things, but not saying them outright. This passive-aggressive resentment can build up, without your ever being aware of it.

If you think through the solution you were about to raise at that meeting, the one where you were so rudely cut off, take an extra moment to construct a non-threatening opening remark, such as one you might have to make in a collectivist cultural setting. Instead of starting with "when I lived in Russia ..." you might consider phrasing your remark as a simple suggestion–such as "Have we considered..."–and refrain from mentioning where you were when you learned this useful morsel. It means, like a carpenter, you measure twice to cut once successfully, only do so with your words, and take time to construct a response that disarms colleagues who might otherwise fire off reflex remarks that reek of competitive resentments.

For some of you, despite thinking carefully before speaking, the process becomes too weighty and frustrating. You feel invalidated as a contributor, and your enthusiasm turns to bitterness or depression. You clam up at meetings, distance yourself from insensitive people around you, and look for another way to find satisfaction in your work. Colleagues whom you once considered close friends seem distant and no longer understand who you are anymore. They think you have not changed. They assume nothing is different and cannot comprehend your surly moods or reluctance to participate in meetings or other office activities you once would have jumped at. This expectation on their part only adds fuel to your frustration level. How can you begin to explain what you cannot understand yourself?

Smart companies will try to debrief their re-entering workforce. They will try to identify skill areas that have been gained or strengthened and ask the employee how best these might be put to use for the company. Sometimes, with an open forum for such feedback, amazing ideas surface, creative solutions are put on the table, and much time and energy can be saved by simply asking the right questions and listening to the well-considered answers. But the best part of all is seeing the twinkle of excitement in someone's eyes again. Someone who knows what they know matters, and they have rediscovered a key place in the office team.

If you have not reviewed your various inventories or discussed your new strengths with mentors, you are not taking full advantage of the opportunities in front of you. This is a great time to evaluate your satisfaction at work, see how well you are able to apply what you have learned abroad, and determine where you think your skill sets are best suited. You may not always like what you hear, but you may learn something about yourself or something about new opportunities just made for your talents and gifts.

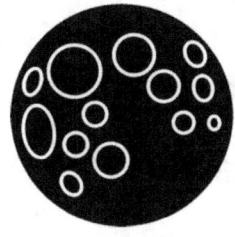

What IS "Home?"

One of the most frequent questions to me is, "When will it *really* feel like home again?" Unfortunately, there is no simple answer to this one. My usual reaction is to respond with the question: *What is "Home" to you?*

The answers are as individual as the people responding, but there are some universal themes, as you may well imagine. To some, Home is a place and the comfortably familiar things that go with that place. To others, Home is a memory of cherished people and the comfortable fit of daily routines together. For many, home is somewhere between those two ideas of physical and emotional comfort and familiarity. Over time, each of us defines Home differently, as we learn more about ourselves and discover what matters most at a given moment in our lives. For me, having lived and worked overseas in so many varied and challenging settings with many different kinds of people, needs, values, and physical contrasts to the senses, Home has come to mean one simple thing: Home is where love is. This sounds very simplistic, but the impact of this discovery was enormous for me. It also means that what Home means to me is not easily understood by many of those around me.

Many re-entry experiences revolve around simple calendar deadlines on paper. Dates to leave the foreign office, close up the rental property and turn off the utilities, close out accounts and return the leased vehicles, collect school and health records, and begin packing up your life abroad. There is perhaps a small personal family vacation or break between leaving one country and coming home again and a start date back at the home office. This can be a blessing for many expats, as the comfort and familiarity of extended family around them again, and, more importantly, on a temporary basis, helps them recapture some sense of what is to come. For others, it can be a smothering and unpleasant side trip, when you realize that you are not the same person anymore, but everyone around you sees you as unchanged and treats you that way too. You may wonder what is wrong with you, and your family may ask frequently if everything is alright. You get tired of the strange looks and can feel people raising their eyebrows and shrugging at one another behind your back. No one knows what's wrong, but everyone can sense something is not right with you.

It is not that something is *wrong* with you; it is that you are *different* from who you were when you last saw these relatives or friends and interacted with them face to face. They still see the same person, hear the same voice, see the same clothing and habits, but they cannot see what is changed in you. You are only just coming to terms with this in yourself–and only if you are observant and very open to self-analysis. Many of us are not. So how do we become more self-aware, better able to identify and understand what is going on within ourselves, and how it affects the people all around us?

What "Home" means is going to change now. As you rediscover yourself back in your home culture or community, you must reassess who you are now and what matters most to you. In some cases, the discoveries you make will play a significant role in all future choices. If you are an employer who has sent someone abroad, this is a great time to debrief your expat and find out what has changed and how it is going to impact your workplace. If you are self-employed, you should take time to assess yourself several times in the coming months or year to make sure your goals are as well aligned with your needs and values as they are now. It is possible to find the agility to respond to these changes in either employment situation. First, though, it must be clearly understood what is being asked and why and what potential changes may come as a result of eliciting this information. For those people or employers unwilling to ask these critical questions, go ahead and keep your head in the sand and see how much it costs you to continue to hide. Things can change in the office—if there is smart and highly adept leadership there. If shared well, the things you have learned can bring immense value to your employer and to your colleagues and customers.

For family or head-in-the-sand employment settings, it may be necessary to bring up the questions yourself. If no one has been through what you have, how can they know what to ask you? Guide them. Share with them. Let them know about some of the more profound lessons learned from your time abroad and how this has made you see the world differently. Only then can true empathy and a strong connection be re-established. People don't stop caring about you just because you seem a bit moody or disconnected from them. But they do have limited patience. You will need to be the one who takes the lead in raising the discussion, but that also gives you control over how broadly or deeply you approach the subject and when. Your initial discomfort will dissolve, as you see the relief in people's eyes, watch their shoulders relax, and see some genuine warmth in their formerly worried gazes. You matter to many people, and if you value these relationships, you will have to work to build a new, redefined Home upon re-entry.

For people moving abroad for longer than a year, many elements of family life can change during the time away. There are variables each family must consider at both ends of the move to determine what's best for them. For example, having another child while abroad may mean more space is required upon the return.

Other families have older children graduating high school and heading off to college or out in the world, no longer in need of a bedroom. Some families may face welcoming aging parents into their homes, and need to have extra space to accommodate this life change. One of the reasons I encourage families to consider selling their homes when they move abroad is because of the sometimes stronger sense of disappointment or detachment they feel when coming back to such a well-remembered place. Nothing will be just as it was, and the sense of loss, of feeling somehow cheated by this failure to recapture precisely what was, can be too powerful for some to accept. The damage done can disrupt family harmony, which of course spills over into the workplace and even onto the kids and their schoolwork. Some families can settle right back in after a few adjustments, but others cannot. There is no way to predict this, but it's a good idea to think through all options.

Letting go of property is a difficult thing. In American culture especially, home ownership is part of the elusive formula defining the American Dream. Of course, in some economies, there are real estate laws, tax issues, and other elements in play that make it impractical or even imprudent to let go of a home. But if you are going to be forever changed by what you experience abroad, it may well be that you will not wish to go back to the way you were living, or even where you were living, when you left.

So now I ask you again, "What is Home to you?"

Make a list. Tell others when it's appropriate. Re-assess as often as necessary. Have the courage to live by the new definition, if at all possible or practical.

What Home means to me...

Home is where love is.

Home is where my favorite books are.

Home is knowing where everything is and how to get to it fast.

These are a few thoughts that come to my mind. What are the things that resonate with you?

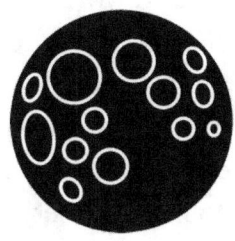

Defining Happiness

This is a big one. Happiness can mean so many things at any given moment in time and space. But we all know when we feel it, and we know when it eludes us. Let's go from there, shall we?

The first lesson of life learned abroad was simple. No one was responsible for your own happiness or misery but you. You quickly learned to detach yourself from maladapted or embarrassingly insensitive expats at the office around you, or you kept your distance by the more socially isolating housing location you chose for yourself, so you and your family wouldn't be sucked into any negative vibes around you. If you didn't do these things, some of you may well wish you had. The important thing is you learned, and you made changes where you could to control or limit the damage. You wanted to do everything you could to ensure your own and your family's happiness.

On one hand, you feel so very lucky that you had had the chance to live and work abroad–something not everyone gets the chance to experience. You had to learn many new ways of doing even the simplest things, since the new culture and physical environment were unfamiliar to you. You were surprised at how small were some of the things you most missed and came to treasure about your former life. You were making new friends, learning what friendship meant in another culture, and how to be a good friend in both your home culture and your host culture settings. It took enormous amounts of energy and time to find a balance between your two worlds. Then it was time to come home.

The delicately attained balance shifted again. If you came back to the same work group, the same home, and got the same furniture out of storage or off a container ship, you may feel somehow pressured to force yourself into the mold of who you were when you left. You make an unconscious effort to recreate all the old routines that were once like functioning on auto-pilot. The people around you–most of whom do not see or feel anything different about you and so they treat you no differently–accept this activity without thought. All is as it was before—or is it?

You may feel a crash, much like a person suffering from depression, when you realize your resumed life is not bringing you any deep satisfaction anymore. You tell yourself it will pass when your body clock adjusts to its old home time zone. You assure yourself that you are worried about your partner or spouse or kids, and once they've settled back in you will be fine too. Keep telling yourself these things. It won't change how you feel. Happiness eludes you, and your inner self is telling you there are many reasons for this and that it will pass. Maybe yes, maybe no.

For some, a gentle depression before finding some semblance of happiness in the good old routine is a comfort. These people may not have other ambitions, dreams, or goals, or have fulfilled these while they lived and worked abroad. Others hunker down, saying little and simply waiting out the time until they can peacefully retire and do what they are dreaming of at a later time.

If you can live with this deferred gratification, then fine. If not, it is time to explore what is behind the feelings. You may need some outside help to get there. This is nothing to be uncomfortable about. In American culture, some of us have so little extended family around us, so few true trusted confidants, we pay to have someone trained to listen and reflect our feelings back at us. Whichever model you live with, you should tell someone what is going on with you. Someone you can trust.

With many expats during re-entry, it is helpful to hook up with others who have been through similar assignments, someone at the office who understands, even without long explanations, what is going on with you. Some companies provide groups and meeting space on company time to see their employees through the first few months back home. Other employers provide professional counseling for couples, families, and, yes, expats. You can specifically request a counselor with actual, personal expat experience, one who can empathize with your situation and issues and not just rely on information gained from an abstract or journal article.

Happiness upon return is attained by clearly understanding who you are now, what you value most in your life, and what you would be doing if you could be doing anything at all, without restriction. Taking these same matters into consideration for your family is crucial, and sharing your feelings and opinions on these issues is worth making time for, no matter how stressful your days. If you can navigate these discussions freely yourself, then do so. If not, seek outside assistance and take pride in knowing that setting your family's happiness and your own as a personal priority is a great commitment.

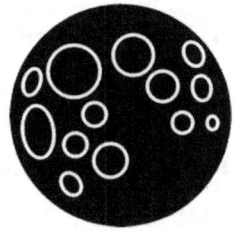

<u>Little Things</u>

Living abroad conjures many memories, some of them nostalgic and others outright hilarious. Overall, though, it is often the tiniest details, the seemingly most insignificant observations, that bring us the most profound joy, satisfaction, or happiness. Walking down an historic street in a city halfway across the planet, a place you'd only seen before in movies, makes you stop and catch your breath with joy and gratitude. The first time you commuted to your new job in your new city abroad and did not get lost or miss the right bus or train, you may have quietly smiled at the sky and pulled a joyfully raised fist back down to your side in celebration. You laughed inwardly at yourself, as you remembered living in a culture that did not value smiling openly at strangers, then you suddenly laughed out loud as people stared at you walking down the street, wondering if you were crazy. The efforts you made to learn a new language, which could make the locals laugh behind charmingly hidden smiles, earned you praise and respect, and, eventually, trust that few like you had ever been awarded.

You missed the taste of the tap water from your kitchen back home or perhaps even the ability to drink directly from a tap. You were horrified the first time you turned on the bath water and looked at something approaching the color of iced tea coming out of the spigot instead. You came to treasure truly bright whites when you did laundry, because your favorite laundry detergent was not available where you were now living. You missed Mexican food, American rules football, or simple conversations with strangers in a checkout line at a grocery store. The bottom line is, some of the things you once thought were essential to your happiness have somehow become less important as you discovered other things about yourself and what constitutes happiness now.

It is important to share these precious self-discoveries and personal adventures when you can, so the people you work with and live with can begin to see how these experiences have changed you and changed how you see yourself. This can be done without a lot of psychoanalysis, especially if you are good at telling stories and describing things and have the ability to laugh at yourself first. Some people are encouraged to create a blog for their family and friends to follow. Others are keen to stay in close contact with mentors and leaders back home, so they have a safe place to land when it's time to come home again. You may want to keep a journal of sorts, both during your time abroad and after you return home to capture the essential memories and lessons learned. In these saved words, you will find the answers to the questions so important to your future happiness.

Trying to define what makes you happy is an ongoing process. We are constantly bombarded with new information and experiences, but we rarely take time to sort through them and ask ourselves what we think of them. Taking time to stop and review our day, and identify what meant the most to us and why, is a good thing. Why not meditate on your day before you sleep each evening, and go over what mattered most. Think about why each small element made you feel the way you did and how more or less important each element is to you. Those little things really add up over time!

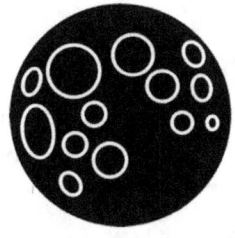

Loss of the Rush

We have all experienced the thrills, challenges, and occasional terror associated with having to learn new things. Imagine your daily life as an expat plotted on a graph with its relative ups and downs from the moment you determined you were going to take this assignment abroad. Once you arrived in-country, you were in a fairly euphoric place, full of excitement and hope, perhaps even confident in your ability to do a great job. After the honeymoon wore off and you were immersed in realities of daily life and having to learn the simplest things in order to live and work successfully there, you viewed things with a more seasoned, realistic eye. You were at the bottom of The Learning Curve, looking up, knowing you had a whole lot of learning in front of you, most of it an upward climb.

Some days, the trip along The Learning Curve was painful, seemingly endless. When would you ever learn that tiny detail about your customer's values that would bring your relationship to that greater level of trust? How could you have worn that dress or suit to a wedding or funeral? Why did no one think to tell you that a color or a certain number was bad luck—or worse? How could you possibly have been expected to know these things?

Even with terrific advance support and preparation, there will always be days when we learn something new about the culture we are in. Over time, some of us gain the ability to identify different values and how they will play out in various cultural settings. We learn, we grow, we make mistakes, we evaluate our mistakes, and we keep on learning. The pride and joy we may take in each small victory on that upward climb, or that advance we made from a recent backward step or two, is profound. The best moments are the ones we get when we feel we've actually mastered something in the target culture. This is the Rush of The Learning Curve. You have worked hard, been highly self-aware—even self-critical at times—to get to these incredible moments.

The biggest bump you may experience on re-entry is the loss of this rush of joy or euphoria in your daily accomplishments. Those myriad little things, and not so little things, you had to learn how to do differently in your new environment brought a lot of moments of success and feelings of pride in your latest discoveries and competencies. Back home again, something in you feels deflated. It's like life on auto-pilot, especially once your home life has settled into a pattern of sorts. Those secret, well-earned puffed-up chests of accomplishment are no more.

It's okay to mourn. It's not okay to wallow. You may not be in a position to change a lot about your life and work at this time, but there are elements of your life that you can change right now. Look at what you miss the most now, and see if there is some part of this prized interest or feeling that you can imitate or recapture by adapting it to your new circumstances. For example, you may have become very fluent in another language. Once home again, you have little or no opportunity to use it. What actions can you take to change that? You might join a club, subscribe to a cable or satellite TV channel, or search the Web for broadcasts in your rusting language. You could stay connected with people in your host country, create a book club together, and stay in touch with a focused reason to connect and talk about issues that still matter to you.

At work, you may feel walled in, or, worse, as if your independent wings have been severely clipped. All of a sudden, those standard weekly team meetings may make you feel like a choke chain has been tightened around your neck. If your overseas office had a smaller staff and you had to broaden your skills quickly to be successful there, now you may find yourself having to remember how to operate on a much narrower spectrum of tasks. This may feel frustrating in the extreme and even create some unexpected and unwelcome conflicts at work, as you inadvertently step on toes of colleagues who feel you are overstepping your job description.

Be gentle with yourself. It took time and patience and a lot of learning to adapt to life abroad and to eventually find success and happiness there too. It will take time to re-compartmentalize or even unlearn some of the behaviors you acquired overseas. You will have to be extra vigilant about observing people's reactions to your encounters at the office and back in the community at home.

In a sense, I am challenging you to treat coming home as another Learning Curve. Don't make careless assumptions that all is as it was before you left. Just because you kept in touch and people kept in touch with you does not mean you are aware of every subtle element that may have changed in their lives too while you were away. Put those observational skills that you mastered abroad to great use. Notice and act on what other re-entry expats may miss. Those small things make all the difference in how well and how quickly you find happiness again.

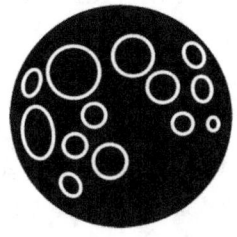

Is *This* All There Is?

In taking on the challenge and eventual mastery in some things on that massive Learning Curve of life abroad, we are enriched in so many ways. The new ways we learned to do things in another culture; the ways we expressed ourselves; the foreign language we worked so hard to function in, the differences in driving, eating, making friends, arguing, and just navigating in a new place–all these lessons are going to have an impact on us for a lifetime. Probably the greatest single lesson is the one where we come to understand that, as much as we are learning and growing, we are still just beginners on the competency scale. It is a humbling realization, but one that keeps us open to observing and learning even more along the journey.

One day, between the Rush of The Learning Curve, the Bump of Re-entry, and settling into life once again back home, the ultimate question comes: Is *this* all there is? It is stunning. We feel horrified at our ungrateful attitude. We are beginning to suffer Sojourner's Guilt. This is a feeling that can hit while you are driving home on your daily commute after a meeting, where you felt frustrated and perhaps even undervalued on your team. Your partner or spouse calls and asks you to pick up some milk and bread on the way home from work. There is nothing new under the sun for you that day. Your life back home is very ho-hum, with no surprises, no Learning Curve staring you in the face. You get home to find your children have had a full and happy day at school or with friends and are immersed in their resumption of a life they couldn't really recall accurately once away from it, but sometimes missed all the same. You envy their simpler—and simply restored—world.

If your spouse or partner was able to return home without employment, the new experiences gained abroad may have a positive and powerful effect on options and future decisions about work and interests in ways your own pre-determined work life cannot.

Your partner may decide to create a whole new kind of job search or decide to go back to school to study and become somebody different in the working world. Be ready for this, and try to be supportive instead of envious. Your older children may also want to make surprisingly mature choices about their own futures; in part, due to the wide range of new experiences your foreign assignment afforded them. By exposure to new ideas and perhaps having more free time to explore options, you may find yourself feeling jealous or even resentful of a family member's freedom to choose, whereas you are feeling slotted into a life that is not what you had hoped it would be. You feel limited, chained, and not full of gratitude. You wonder if there is something more to all this, something you may have missed in the details of coming home again.

These feelings, left unattended, can grow into serious emotional difficulties later on. There is nothing wrong with feeling a sense of letdown once you are no longer living life on a steep and challenging Learning Curve. It's what you *do* to enrich your re-entry experience, once you acknowledge your feelings of restlessness or disappointment, that makes all the difference.

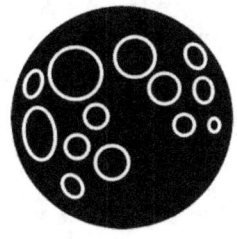

Sojourners Guilt

If you have lived abroad for any significant time, or worked abroad extensively and have learned much along the way, you know you come home each time forever changed. The people, places, memories, and lessons learned are part of you now. There is no way to pretend it all never happened; there is no way to close your mind to all those new ways of thinking, solving problems, looking at life, or dealing with people. You are so fortunate to have had the opportunities you have had. You have so much more to bring to the table in terms of work experiences and communicating across cultures and differences, and it shows. It sounds great, doesn't it? But what about the people around you who have never had any experiences remotely like yours?

Feeling proud of your accomplishments abroad is natural. You have no reason to hide what you have learned, but you may have to learn how to couch your comments and suggestions in language that does not pose a threat to the more competitive, sensitive, or downright envious types around you. It is sad that we must do this. We must mask how we know something or not share all the rich details gained in the learning of what we are about to share at times. We feel guilty that we are doing a disservice to the wonderful cultural mentors and guides abroad who helped us learn these useful things, and we want to give them credit for their generosity.

Occasionally you will be rewarded by your tact when someone approaches you after a discussion and is intrigued with what you'd had to say. They want to know more, and you are then free to acknowledge the source of your enlightenment. It feels wonderful, and it usually reminds you how long it's been since you took time to contact that person and re-connect. Do it! They will be flattered and touched to hear of their impact on your life at home again.

When you agreed to take a foreign assignment and move your life to another country, you affected not only your family life, but your work life and your position in each of your communities, however you define them. It is unfair and unrealistic to assume you can blithely take up where you left off. Taking yourself out of those real-time settings and communicative equations had a price. Relationships continued to flourish without you there, decisions were made without your input, and life moved on without you, possibly in directions you would not approve or support. Perhaps a beloved relative died while you were living too far away to join in the grieving in a more personal way. Family members left behind while you were abroad may have some feelings about it long after you return home. Comments made thoughtlessly, in the heat of a moment, cannot be withdrawn. Resentments may surface, if work team or family squabbles contain ongoing content that you were not there for. Your comments now may cause tension if you are unaware of the deeper context of a conversation. Try first to be a very good listener and observer when you get home. Re-enter each of your communities, whether workplace, family, religious, sports, or other types of hobby and interest groups, with the goal of catching up without interfering or jumping in too soon. Until you are sure of the atmosphere, don't step out into it.

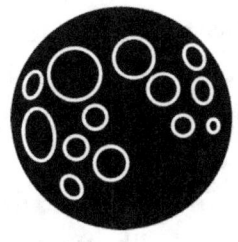

Family First

From the moment you came home from work, dazed at your offer to move abroad, excited but wondering how to break it to your partner and family, you have probably done everything humanly possible to put your family's needs before your own, right? If not, you may have been on the receiving end of emotional backlash from family members that has damaged your relationships and influences your own feelings about your work.

Sometimes, as counter-intuitive as it may seem, it pays to put your family first, before your own professional and personal needs and goals. For some, especially men and women who are socialized into the role of caretaker, this is not such a challenge. For others who may have been raised to produce, perform, earn, and take downtime when possible to let off steam from all the competitive and performance pressure, it is not something easily or naturally done. You know I'm speaking to you now. Don't duck and cover. You need to think this one through.

For families who really made the initial decision to go abroad as a team, the transition home again will probably be equally as cooperatively accomplished. If, however, you were one who was in the alpha position to provide, decide, and execute, dragging your family along for the duration, willing or not, you may want to take some time and evaluate the impact re-entry is going to have on each family member, even the ones awaiting you back home.

Let's start with the family back home, since they are already in place and not in transition as you are. Your parents, closer siblings, and even dear friends who may be more like family to you than your own blood relations, may have certain expectations about your return. If you have aging parents who can no longer travel comfortably or safely, the issue of where to settle, who is primary caregiver, and so forth, all are looking you in the eye for consideration. You and your partner or spouse may want to do some serious long-range planning for your future together. You might be shocked to discover that you've been thinking about where to retire and how you envision your lifestyle, only to find your partner has totally different ideas about this time of your life together. So start talking about this, no matter what your age. Moving is costly, and as long as the company is paying for it, you would be wise to think things through as carefully as possible, to make the most efficient use of the opportunity. Do you really want to move back into your old house, the one you may have been renting out while abroad? Might it be time to downsize, relocate closer to parents, or others you want to remain in close contact with?

Think about the following housing and lifestyle issues:

• In your time abroad, did you choose to experiment with a different kind of housing than what you were used to?

• Did you move from a larger single-family home to a smaller flat, condo, or duplex?

• What were your experiences living abroad? Was it just a temporary adventure to try living another way? Are you ready to go back to what was, or are you thinking about trying something different?

• What did you learn about yourself and any family members who may have gone along with you?

• Have you ascertained what everyone is thinking about the return move?

• What are your preferences now, when you think about commuting time, distance to the office, the gym, and other variables?

• Are there health, age or other constraints that must be factored into your housing decisions?

• If you have children who were schooled abroad, what kind of educational setting might be best for them upon your return, and why?

• What does your partner or spouse think about all of this, and what are you doing to clearly communicate and share these important discoveries?

You may have begun living abroad with the intent to test out something new, but hopefully you are open enough to evaluate whether you have learned something unexpected about yourselves in the process and can use this newly acquired knowledge about personal lifestyle preferences to make good decisions about your re-entry.

Talking openly about these feelings is the only way to move forward. Until life is perfect, it is expected some compromises will have to be made, but by whom? Issues like weather, health, fuel prices, commuting distances, public transit, access to necessities and services, religious communities, hobbies, parking, schools, and the general cost of living should all factor into your discussions.

You might be surprised to find that, after your kids have been in schools abroad, they might have a heck of a readjustment to a neighborhood public school with a more crowded classroom and a more or less advanced math and science curriculum. If you had been in contact with your local school district or curriculum specialist before your departure abroad, you may have brought relevant classroom materials with you on assignment to supplement and otherwise keep up with the home academic requirements.

Many nations, for example, lack the creative writing and speech and communications curricula so prevalent in U.S. schools. Kids may return home at a deficit, if no one has encouraged them to keep up these skills. If you are one of these families, you may want to begin a journaling program with your children and come together after dinner once in a while to talk about their entries, modeling good communication back to them, after reviewing their writing talents. You also want to encourage your children to collect and store accurate contact information for their new friends, so they can begin keeping in touch remotely if they choose. You may have already done this in reverse by setting up a social networking account, blog, or website of your family's time abroad so you didn't have to constantly answer messages one at a time. Coming home so school-age kids can have a summer to reacquaint themselves to life back home again is a wonderful thing if you can arrange it. If you are moving to a different community, summer breaks give time to make new friends and get the lay of the land before arriving at school as a "new kid." There are also more houses on the market in the U.S. during this window

(April-August) than any other time of year, so pickings are more plentiful.

What about a spouse or partner? What kinds of concerns do they have? Are they leaving behind another job abroad and having to start all over to follow you somewhere new? If this is the case, perhaps you can ask your employer if there is any job-finding assistance provided due to income lost during the transition. A smart employer knows that financial stress is a serious cause for household discord. By investing a smaller sum in worker transition assistance for your partner, the employer may find you more positive and highly productive as a result of experiencing more support and less stress during this sometimes challenging process of re-entry. The cost to the employer is minimal compared to losing your talents due to having to relocate to accommodate a spouse or partner's unassisted job search that brings in offers far from your employer's location.

If you are proactively reading this before accepting an overseas assignment, consider negotiating this type of partner or spousal assistance into your contract. Some companies are even so generous as to incorporate a stipend for lost wages in countries where a partner will be unable to apply for a work visa. If they really need you, it can't hurt to ask.

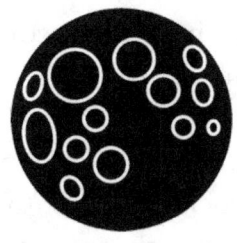

Backlash

Have you ever tried to do the right thing, only to find it coming back in your face? Backlash is the result of not thinking something through as well as you could have, perhaps acting in haste or excitement, when stopping and thinking might have better served you. Moving abroad is one of those decisions that can be fraught with backlash consisting of often completely unintended and unforeseen consequences. You may not have realized until you arrived abroad that not everyone in the family or on your work team had been equally committed to, or interested in, your making this move. While some people may cover up their feelings better than others, eventually some of their unhappiness will find its way to you. But beware—backlash can strike in both directions of your move. Just because your employer dictates, or *your* employment opportunity abroad is coming to a close, it does not necessarily mean the timing for another move is good for your spouse or partner and your other family members.

Your re-entry can have many consequences at home with family and friends, with your partner or spouse, with your children, as well as with your co-workers, mentors, and other significant people in your life. Think of your own life as a rock thrown into a pond. Watch the ripples circle out across the surface of the water. Each decision you think you can make on your own is going to touch others whether you wish it or not. The surprise will be how far out the ripple effect goes, not that it exists. Let's look at this pattern in both a workplace and a personal context.

In the foreign office, you have been learning many new things, things you hope will eventually bring great value to the team waiting back home. But while you were away, other people were also gaining skills, making career choices, seeking mentors, and developing valuable relationships, sometimes with people who also know you well and value your talents. Unless you have been keeping in close contact with your home team, you may have been making a lot of assumptions about your re-entry career plans that no longer fit the present office scenario. Budget cuts, new leadership, loss of a major client account, any or all of these variables may suddenly shift, leaving you without a clue as to what your return to the workplace back home will look like. Keeping in touch and keeping up takes effort and time, and unless you have made time for this, you are going back blind. Your assumptions might make others feel resentful, as if your return is an annoyance, one that causes everyone to have to stop, shift gears, and catch you up on what's been happening and what is being done to address office challenges. Your confident manner, easy leadership, and open communication style may generate glares behind your back. You may be happy to return to the home office but impervious to the fact that not everyone is happy to see you there, especially the person who was hoping to step into *your* new position. Backlash.

On the home front, your family may be feeling everything from relief or sadness about going home again to outright resentment that, once again, you are destroying their lives and they have no choice in the matter. This last is a common, dramatic response from teens leaving peers, terrified of being the odd-one-out back home, or in some new location, where they have no place in the hierarchy yet. This is also why it pays to try to move during a summer, when older children have a chance to slowly feel their way into new relationships without hallway cliques and classroom settings. Younger children will be a bit more cuddly and even regress in some behaviors, much as they did on the way out. Restless sleep, nightmares, and even backsliding on toileting habits are common in such a stressful time in a young life. If you have a spouse or partner who is primarily dealing with the kids while you waltz off to the office, get ready for the updates when you get in the door each day after work. You are definitely resting on the easier end of the stick on this one. Try to listen, remain patient, and offer support as best you can. Bringing home a favorite dinner could earn big points!

If your partner is in a decent mood, try to share a bit about what you are experiencing at the home or office, so you both come to understand that each person's re-entry has its own challenges, and this is not a contest. But wait, there's more! With your extended family waiting back home, some dynamics may have changed because you were no longer as frequently or as deeply involved with decisions on aging parents and other timely discussions. What you see as your place in your extended family may have changed, and the traditions and routines to expect may no longer exist. A sibling may have stepped into your role, and adjustments will have to be made to accommodate your return. This will take time. Again, you must be patient. Your decision to move abroad is what caused this ripple effect. You cannot simply step back in and take up right where you left off. The sting of backlash awaits if you do.

To the spouses and partners of the re-entering employees, have a heart. It is not easy to go back to a work setting that is no longer operating precisely as it was when you left. There are many nuances that will elude your loved one for a time and many conversations to catch up on that they were not part of, but somehow are constantly expected to know about and act on. There may be days when your partner comes in the door, and you can feel there is something wrong, but nothing is said. Don't let these solitary sighs and down days go by without addressing them. At least make an effort to discover what's causing them. Assure your partner you are also there to listen. Sometimes in simply sharing a burden, a solution comes to us while we are talking or listening. Other times, it is generous to ask for another's perspective instead of holding it in and feeling lost or depressed about things over which you feel you have no control. This is a step toward taking control of your re-entry circumstances and mitigating the backlash.

One of the more painful lessons–and a reason why many expats do not choose to move back into their old residences–is the occasional discovery that you are so changed by your experiences abroad that you no longer have much in common with your old neighbors. These terrific people who were sorry to see you leave and happy to welcome you home again do not necessarily realize how out of place you may be feeling back "home." The things you've learned, the places you've been, the formerly acceptable ideas you've had challenged by your experiences abroad, all this has contributed to the new you. You may have learned a new skill or language, taken up a new sport or hobby, or decided to live in a completely different type of housing after your expatriate exposure. If you are going back to your old home, give it time. Some people find they can settle in again just fine over time. Others need to re-evaluate their living situation a year later and have some deep discussions about how they are feeling and what they would like to be doing instead. Either start the conversation or participate in it, but don't avoid it. Backlash.

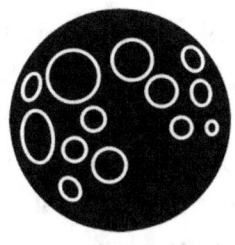

Not the Same Me

Once you are home again, your temper, feelings of impatience and frustration, moments of depression or anger for what was lost–all these are symptoms of change and your response to it. That incredible Learning Curve you urged yourself to climb and, occasionally, master, was such an undertaking! The things you've learned and unlearned about yourself, about life, about the world and how it works–all of this has had a profound impact on you. You thought being an expat meant working abroad and getting a chance to see a bit more of the world. It did, of course, but it was also so much more.

Sometimes the responses of others are your first clue that you yourself are different. People who knew you before your move abroad, people with whom you've tried to keep in touch, might find themselves confused or surprised by some of your behavior or responses these days. These awkward interactions can come in both business and personal settings, so let's look at how many of them can play out.

Since it pays the bills, let's begin by exploring a workplace scenario. Your boss might call you into the office for a chat, and the turn of conversation may surprise you. It won't be about work, it will be about *you*. Relax, this doesn't mean you're in trouble. It means that someone cares about you and has noticed that you are not as easily understood as you once were. It's time to open up and share, whether you are comfortable doing so or not. If your boss has lived or worked abroad, the conversation may be very meaningful almost as soon as you both start talking. If not, you will need to be patient and explain how you feel about the work before you and how you can best contribute, perhaps by putting some of the newly acquired skills to work for the team.

It's important to let your boss or mentors know your state of mind, your potential contributions to the company, and any ideas that may prove beneficial to the company as a whole. This is not easy to do, nor should it be done in haste. Think things through, and try to put as positive a spin on things as possible, avoiding negative comments or criticism about colleagues. After all, they don't know what you know, and you don't know what they've been doing without you. Tread carefully, listen well, and when it is time to speak, offer suggestions using team-based terms like *we, us, our*, and *ours*.

The workplace dynamic is very similar to what it will feel like to re-establish old ties with friends, family, and neighbors. Yes, the burden is mostly on you, since you are the one who left, and you are the one most changed. Talk with your family about these feelings. Be sure to debrief your partner or spouse and any children old enough to verbalize their feelings. If anyone is having trouble settling in again, there is nothing to be uncomfortable about. If talking it through together does not seem helpful enough, then seek outside expertise. If you think someone in the family is suffering from clinical depression or is unable to cope with re-entry, don't wait. Get help.

If you are employed with health benefits, you probably have access to terrific psychological counseling. Try to find someone who's been an expat. While not crucial, it can make the introductory conversations that much shorter, almost telegraphic, as you get to work on feeling at home again. Keep reminding yourself that, much like having a baby, it's a long process to learn to live another way. Also like having a baby, life is never the same again. Things will not just bounce right back to what they were before. It will take time to reacquaint yourself to life at home, even though the people around you perceive little or no difference in you until a specific sensory experience, event, or decision triggers a reaction in you they were not expecting.

You will become better at observing the responses of people around you by monitoring yourself and, if you brought a family along for your journey, your family. Try to allow time after work each day to reach out and listen to how your family is settling in, what they have experienced, and how it has affected them. Sometimes the smallest thing can set off a crying jag, a longing for life abroad again, or a sigh of remembered contentment thought forever lost. One member of your family, just as when your trip abroad began, will adapt more quickly than the rest. It's not a contest, and there is no typical timeline you can hold up to compare against your own progress. Each person interacted differently with the setting abroad, and each will feel joy, despair, nostalgia, regret, and contentment uniquely. In fact, because we each respond differently at re-entry, the variations in personal timelines allow us to care for one another as each goes through the sometimes nearly painless, or occasionally highly painful, process.

Many expats in high-level or high-visibility positions at work often comment they have too little time to indulge in re-entry issues. While the pressures of work may seem heavy, particularly if you feel you are struggling to catch up on everything that's going on around you, it is critical that you make time to acknowledge you are going through something. Let your family help you over the hump days if you believe you cannot let yourself "show" your re-entry moods and feelings at work. To deny what you are going through only makes even more people around you notice something is not right. Eventually you either settle in again, maybe not exactly in the same way as before, and you find a level of satisfaction, or you realize you no longer fit this environment and need to make a change of some kind. You are not alone.

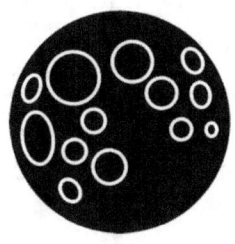

Underappreciated & Undervalued (The Other Offer)

Change is all around you. Change is in you. Why can't others simply recognize this and work with you until you find happiness again? The hardest thing to notice when we are feeling badly ourselves is that we are not the only ones who feel this way. A lot of the time, when you are feeling like no one understands you at work anymore, no one seems to care what you think when you try to speak up at a meeting, you become frustrated, impatient, and even angry. Your children, your spouse or partner, chances are they are also going through similar experiences. Tempers may be running hot at home. Talking things out is half the battle to taking control of the situation. But you have to find a state of mind to be able to do so in a civilized and thoughtful manner. You know, choose your battles, and if you do speak up, be ready to listen at least as well to what others have to say. This is easier said than done, of course, because you must find a semblance of calm and control in order to truly listen, share, and try to understand and be understood.

For spouses or partners, don't be surprised if, one evening out of the blue, your mate comes home, dumps his briefcase on the couch, stomps over to a chair and mutters that work is no fun anymore. You've both learned so many new things, often under a lot of pressure and constraints, and now it seems life around you is supposed to be lived as though it all never happened. You cannot unmake who you are now as a result of all those experiences you shared abroad, and you cannot understand why people don't seem to care about what is important to *you*. Why can't they see it? How can you possibly explain it? When you try, people clam up or reject what you are trying to say, not even giving you a chance. It hurts, and it causes you to feel unappreciated. You feel you're not bringing value to the work or the team anymore. This can feel depressing, even suffocating.

At work, on community service boards and committees, in the diverse social settings to which we all return, there are times when what we say is simply ignored or overlooked. Perhaps we did not phrase it well? Did we unintentionally step on some erstwhile leader's toes?

Or there are those times we are using a behavior we learned to value in that other place, far from where we are now, and people look at us as if we are crazy. These are all common experiences and, over time, they may diminish as we settle in again. Or not.

Each of us chooses what we will retain of ourselves from before and after our expatriate experience. We may not think it through to any great degree, but we do come to a point of comfort in ourselves with our values and how we live them. Once home again, the trouble is that not everyone around us understands what we have acquired and how it can affect us in our interactions. We may not even notice these often minute changes in ourselves, but the signals of frustration we emit and receive are obvious. This is when the restlessness comes into play for some re-entry sojourners. How will you choose to handle it?

For some, the answer lies in sharing what's going on with you with a trusted mentor, colleague, or other confidant whom you respect. If there is a way to improve the workplace situation by confidential discussions and actions, you may be able to settle into your former job and adapt to the new you in the adjusted circumstances. If you are not able to communicate, adapt, and have the impact you wish to at work, then it's time for a change. Sometimes the change can be within the same company; sometimes it's time to move on. Many times, it's knowing how much you came to appreciate the loss of The

Learning Curve, since you miss the rush of daily challenges to master new things. You may have met some influential people in your time abroad. If you were thorough in your bridge-building or gardening skills, you would have kept in touch with them. They may very much want to bring you onto their team, since they have seen you in action in an expatriate setting. It can be very flattering and exciting, but is it a good move?

If you are a proactive reader, you might use this knowledge to plan well ahead. The hope is that you will never need to make a move due to unhappiness at work back home again. Should you chance to meet wonderful and interesting people while abroad, do make the effort to keep precise contact records, and take the time to build the relationships, if they bring you pleasure. You never know who is going where next and how your skills, contacts, talents, and personality may be just the perfect fit for what is to come. Losing track of these potentially valuable people or opportunities is foolish. Who knows? It could even be you needing them someday, right?

If this discussion sounds like something you've been facing at work or with your partner or spouse, get ready. The next step is often a surprise for the one who's settled in fairly well again, though it doesn't have to be now you've been warned. The contacts you've made the effort to keep in touch with may come through with an incredible, irresistible offer to head abroad again, this time to an even more exciting location, at a very tempting salary. Don't jump at it too fast, and be sure to give your family time to absorb the possibilities. If there are teens in the mix at home, heading out again just after returning and making new friends is not a tempting scenario. You may have to do some creative problem-solving to meet everyone's needs, but it can be done if you really feel happiness lies elsewhere.

To the corporate leaders and future leaders who may take time to read this, what are you doing to cultivate the most value from your returning expats? How are you assessing what their strengths are now? How will you best retain and use them for maximum gain all around? Use them or lose them.

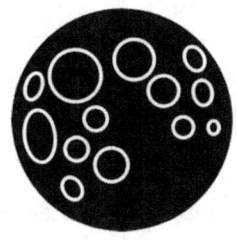

Re-entry Enrichment Strategies

Whether you are self-employed and just want a guiding light through the jolts of re-entry, or you are a corporate manager or leader looking for solutions, there are things you can do. Not everything has to cost money. Most well-considered approaches in life require thought, information, planning, execution, and evaluation on an ongoing basis. Not all of this has to cost money, but it will take time, energy, and commitment. Are you willing to explore this thoroughly enough to make a difference? If not, stop reading now, put down the book, and pass it along to someone who will use it well. Don't waste your own time.

If you have observed there are losses in your organization, potentially due to re-entry issues, or you are a solo sojourner who is feeling out of place back home, and especially at work, even after giving it time and trying a few new things to change it up a bit, then you do need to keep reading. Something is missing in your re-entry experience, and if you can put your finger on it, you may just be able to do something about it. The biggest single deficit in most repatriation scenarios is simple: *re-entry is a process, but few discern this or treat it as such*. The first step to creating solutions is to isolate the issues and identify which of these is the most critical (this can vary depending on settings and people involved) at the time for each expat, family, or work situation. This is a great time to take out some paper or sit at your computer and jot down a few thoughts, things only you will see and know about for now. Sometimes it is not smart to open up to others until you are comfortable with how you are feeling and how you can best communicate these ideas.

For solo acts, take a look at every aspect of your life as it is now. Go through a work day and a non-work day. Try to list the elements that make up your days in a table, including the fun and the less-fun aspects of each. Think back to your life abroad after you have done this. Then try to re-create the elements of both work and non-work days abroad. Look for overlapping patterns between the lists you have made from then and now. Next, you must be brave. Step out and dream a little. Mark the elements of each life you like best. What things make you feel best about yourself, and why?

This will take some time, and you do not want to be disturbed when you do this so you can remain strongly focused and on-task. This exercise is wonderful if you are a high-detail thinker and like to examine things closely. For those of us who are more bigger-picture thinkers, who may not be patient with the details of life, this exercise is a serious challenge, but one that can help enormously in getting to the heart of the matter. Why does your life seem to feel "less" than it was before or somehow empty compared to when you were abroad? Once you start marking off the elements you enjoy most on both sections of the table, patterns will emerge.

You may see a great deficit in the way your life is operating now compared to what you just left while living and working abroad. Whether those elements were viewed by you as positive or negative, they were part of your psyche each day, and the behaviors and emotions and experiences were things you became very familiar with and came to identify as part of yourself, or yourself abroad.

Corporate global mobility experts can easily see how a model like this could be applied across the company by de-briefing every expat employee and spouse or partner who wishes to participate in the process. Some companies may have counselors or psychological specialists to take on this work and report back to the company, though this exercise is so private, so personal an exploration, it is probably best done alone. Partners can come together and share their findings, but only after first determining where each stands on before-and-after life abroad issues in private. Experts can be useful in guiding people through the process and holding them accountable to get it done and face up to the results. Individuals can decide whether they want broad or limited types of assistance through this process, if any.

Some expats find deficits in areas that completely catch them off guard. Things like housing, space, commuting, and even the work space at the office–all these can generate dissatisfaction in life upon re-entry, if how you were living abroad was something you came to value greatly, often without realizing it once you came home again. This is why you must ask yourself the tough questions.

Imagine a family who started out in a metropolitan suburb of a large city, living in a single-family home with a large lawn and garden to care for. The same family moved abroad to a more central urban location and chose to live in an elegant apartment in a trendy part of that city and commuted to work just a few minutes per day on an underground rail system, instead of sitting in a car in traffic. They could walk to shops, eat out, or pick up a paper in moments, just outside their apartment entrance. There was no lawn or garden to care for, and they could travel on weekends. The work was satisfying, but the lifestyle and the chance to see more of the world might have been an even larger enticement to go abroad in the first place; it wasn't about the money or a promotion for this family. Then it was time to come back to the same suburban house they left, the same lawn and garden, the same commute, the same job and work team.

With this example for comparison, if you take the time to write out the elements for both before and after you lived and worked abroad, you can easily see where some of the hardest jolts of re-entry could hit. What is not so easily seen is that just because you are returning to a previous life, replicated and restored to almost exactly what it had been before your departure, you may no longer *prefer* living that way. This experience is almost insidious, because common sense tells us we had a pretty good life just the way it was, thank you very much. To come back to it, intuitively, one would think it would be a relief to fall naturally into patterns easily recaptured, valued friendships taken up from where they left off, and return to a work group with whom you'd been in nearly constant contact the whole time anyway.

And for some expats on re-entry, it does happen just that way. After a few months of discomfort, like getting a new pair of jeans broken in, we hit a time when things simply feel like they fit again. As they mostly fall back into quiet place, we move forward, much as we had done before. But not all of us fall into this category, and that's okay too. It's what we do about it when we make this discovery that matters most.

You may have determined that elements such as the weather, the traffic, the kitchen in your home, the carpeting instead of the wooden floors you got used to abroad, all seem to bother you now. Change them if after a time you still feel this way, but first you must be sure to share with your inner circle that you are thinking of making some changes. Think about it. Weather might require that you move elsewhere or modify things about your living space that recreate what you miss now. Traffic issues or how something is designed in your present domicile might require you to relocate to other quarters in order to gain that missing element that seemed to bring you so much enjoyment. Be sure of what is driving your deficits and your actions. Don't let self-deceptive thoughts and actions steer you away from finding happiness again. Nothing can fix what's broken without a diagnostic process to determine an underlying cause.

So after you've completed your self-survey, ask yourself which things are the most crucial. Then ask yourself why.

• Is there some deeper reason behind your unhappiness or dissatisfaction?

• Is your partner or spouse having a hard time finding a job, and money problems are really underlying all the reasons you are citing?

• Is your spouse or partner having an easier time at re-entry than you are, and this is what's really bothering you?

• Are there children involved, and is one or more not having an easy time of it?

• Is your job back home not nearly as glamorous or as independently worked as it was abroad?

• Is there a pattern, a hobby, or other repeated activity from life abroad that you miss more than you thought, and cannot replicate or adapt it for life back home?

Why not pull back a bit, give yourself some distance from your lists, and evaluate whether time is all that's needed to settle in again or whether you really need to sit down and talk out what's not right with you these days. What's the worst that could happen? You've shared that you are going through something that's hard to pin down, and you need space to think and evaluate. By informing people who care about you, they are going to cut you some slack if at all possible and not push you too hard if you go inward for a time. They know only you can answer these questions, and only time will allow you to see the answers for yourself.

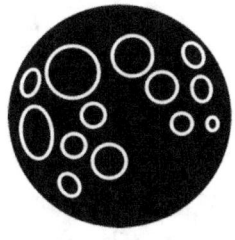

Closer Than Ever...or Not

Many successful military families discover a certain, special closeness that other civilian families may never experience, and much of this comes from frequent relocation. The military family deployed elsewhere every few years either survives, possibly even strengthens, or perishes from the stress of picking up and starting over, and over, and over. Not everyone is so flexible. Conditions in different locations vary so greatly as to create additional stress. Quality of education, available jobs on and off base, types of housing, weather, access to cultural amenities, and so forth–all these variables shift with each move, not to mention cultural differences in each community that must be faced, learned about, and mastered before having to move on again. This life is not for everyone, nor does everyone get through it happily or successfully. The same is true of expat families.

Advice I often give to couples outbound on assignment for the first time is this: if you have any areas of friction in your relationship now, they will be amplified greatly by moving abroad. This is not a time to ignore what is wrong in a marriage or a job. Moving away from where you are now will not change these problems. You cannot escape them, but you can magnify them by throwing the stress of such a move into the mix. Choose carefully what matters most to you, and make your decisions accordingly.

I say precisely the same thing to couples heading home again. Have some areas of friction been revealed or created by your move abroad? Perhaps a spouse or partner was unable to obtain a work visa and had always set great store by what he or she does for a living, and the loss of work became a loss of identity. There would be a load of resentment to deal with there and much to focus on to try to restore what was lost once you return home again. Are you willing and able to put this need before others you face? So it's time to make another list, but this time, do it together.

As a couple, work to discover what you have most come to appreciate about your life together abroad. Also look frankly at what you have missed most or what you have come to enjoy that is different from your life before you left. If there are children involved, also look at how successful or unsuccessful they have been during this experience and what needs they have that must be addressed and how best to do this. You may end up with a lengthy wish list of preferences, needs, and priorities.

It may surprise you to discover many things on your list were not part of life before you moved abroad. You may want to share relevant factors with your boss or manager, and see if where you return to, work-wise, can accommodate some of these elements. This is not easy if you are employed by a huge corporation that has slotted you in somewhere. If you are employed by a multi-site employer, and you have smartly remained in close contact with key mentors and movers in the company, this is a great time to reach out and see what else might open up for you. If you are self-employed, this is a great opportunity to look around for a good fit on as many aspects as possible to suit your entire family's needs, including your own.

One interesting aspect of life abroad is how your older children respond to the re-entry. If you took high school-age children with you, they may well return home and head off as independently as possible, to "catch up with their peers." In countries where the age to consume alcohol is much younger than your home country, having to give up alcohol will be frustrating. Your teen may feel like rebelling on this, so have a plan in place to deal with the fallout, before a police officer shows up at your door one night and your stomach rolls in terror. The inverse is true with driving. Very often, Americans allow children to drive at younger ages than other nations. Coming back to the chance to drive, when peers may have been doing so for years already, can make parents very uneasy. Address this deficit as quickly and as firmly as possible to avoid any unchangeable outcomes.

You may find your children have matured in many ways beyond their age-grade peers, again depending on your home life and the culture in which they've been immersed, and how teens are treated. On the other hand, American teens are often far more precocious and independent in many ways than teens from many other nations, and their age-grade peers abroad may have an innocence about them that is charming, but are different enough to create social chasms. Look carefully at what your child's life has been like abroad. Take time to talk about their hopes, dreams, and plans for the future. Keep these things in mind as you build a new life at home again. To ignore these issues can mean causing deep fractures in the family structure.

Academics abroad is a huge issue with lifetime impact on children. What kind of educational setting were they in abroad? Were there deficits in the curriculum, such as in math, science, or creative writing? Were the sports programs so different that the sport does not exist back home? Is your child very advanced or lagging behind in some areas; if so, what type of school will you need to select in order to strengthen your child's experience? In many families, accelerated learning abroad in math and the sciences is common, but often deficits exist in oral and written communication and literature. Can the school you select accommodate these differences in achievement by subject? Take time to talk with school administrators and counselors, and speak with the subject matter teachers when you share records.

Often some kind of cultural translation will be required, and you are the only one knowledgeable.

If you are reading this before you move abroad, then be proactive about purchasing age-grade appropriate materials, or electronic access to them, from the school or district you are most likely returning to, so your child can keep up by doing extra work. If you start the pattern early while abroad, before making friends occurs, you will have built a good habit for a lifetime.

So, closer together as a family or not? Many expatriate couples and families report a sort of honeymoon phase when they first go abroad, before the challenge of life with a daily, uphill Learning Curve hits them. If you can master that with each other, you can hold everyone together through the burn of re-entry. For many, the re-entry bumps and bruises are stronger, hurt more, and have longer-lasting effects if untreated. We expect life will be different on the way out. We do not naturally assume life will be even more different on our return. Or is it we who are different?

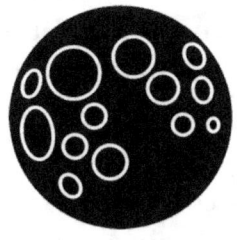

Here We Go Again

People laugh when they are told, even before their departure abroad, that it is likely a good number of them will want to head out on another expatriate assignment within twenty-four months of their return. What they don't know about yet is that "Rush of The Learning Curve." The adrenaline rush of terror-turned-to-triumph as elements about the new life abroad are discovered, explored, and eventually even mastered or understood and valued. We see some evidence of this in our brave military men and women, many of whom are not home very long before signing up for another tour of duty in what the puzzled loved ones at home see as tough, primitive, dangerous, terrifying, and even deadly conditions.

Why would anyone want to leave home? Don't you remember hearing that when you first told family and friends you had accepted a transfer abroad? You understand now that not everyone can do what you have chosen to do. Not everyone wants to, or needs to, leave home to see and learn about what the world can be like far from home. But you may need to.

What you have learned about yourself and the world around you can never be taken from you. But you can and will lose the rush of The Learning Curve unless you can get that near-constant sense of challenge and accomplishment in other ways. For some, you may find a semblance of this need fulfilled by learning a new sport, relocating domestically, or finding a new job in a completely new place, but one where your family is not so challenged as they might be by living abroad again. For others, none of these options is sufficient to fulfill the driving need to recapture feeling the most alive you have felt in your life. Talk it over with your partner and with your employer. Sometimes your partner may also be feeling the same way and is relieved that you brought it up first. Then the solution is easy, and you can address it together. Your employer may surprise you and may have just been waiting to see how you were settling in before approaching you to uproot yourself, and possibly your family, once again. Your achievements abroad may have had such a positive impact on your company that you are seen as a key player in global growth now.

Some of you may find that bringing up the topic of another potential move abroad is not well received. Your partner or spouse may have just found the dream job of a lifetime and is not happy contemplating pulling up roots again after just growing some new ones. You may have older children who are close to graduating from high school, and they have made plans that require holding still a while. If this is the case, perhaps there is room for some flexible or creative solutions. For that spouse who cannot obtain a work visa abroad, there are many options for self-employment that can work within the parameters of the foreign setting. Some choose to build network marketing companies based on strong personal relationships, with funds flowing into domestic accounts, avoiding any conflicts with foreign government regulations. Others take time to study further, often at employer expense, as recompense for income lost by the move.

For those older children, there are incredible boarding schools and university programs now that welcome high school students with excellent grades, emotional maturity, and strong study skills to come and learn in an accelerated high school diploma/bachelor's degree program. Or those children may want to come along, take a year off after completing high school, and learn about the world around them before deciding what they want to do with their lives. How many high school graduates enter higher education programs clueless as to why they are studying and what they plan to do? Maybe that extra time could help them find an answer and provide better motivation and focus when they do finally register to study further.

In the case of very strong, committed families and relationships, there can be choices made that call for sacrifice on the one hand, so joy and happiness can be found by half of the partnership. This is a difficult topic, because not every relationship can withstand this type of separation. In this model, the employee or contractor who's received the offer to go abroad again feels it is something simply too incredible to pass up. The rest of the family does not feel the same way. They have settled in again and have found a rhythm to their lives that they are okay with. They have no need to experience the rush of The Learning Curve again. Once was enough. But it was not enough for one family member, who has just been offered the most incredible opportunity. This person is excited enough about it to bring it home and tell you—as opposed to hiding it and saying nothing—even though they know you are not in agreement. So it matters very much to this person. *Listen.*

Even though one of you may not want to, couples in this situation have to talk it through. Very often, though, there is a decision deadline that is coming up very fast. Foreign assignments can sometimes crop up very quickly in response to an urgent and recently determined customer need or competitive trend that suddenly changed. The bad news is that time to make a choice is very limited. The good news is that you have leverage. If an employer needs you somewhere now, and no one else can get the job done as well as you, then you have room to make some demands, ones that can accommodate some of your family's needs. Perhaps you want to accept another assignment abroad, but your family would prefer to remain back home. Negotiate for travel benefits with a frequency and duration your family can live with. Talk it over. Make a list and review it carefully. Some elements you may want to consider:

- How do you wish to live? House, apartment, cottage, mansion, farm, etc.
- How close to work do you prefer to live?
- What kind of transportation needs will you have?
- What is the Cost of Living difference from where you are now? If the next location is significantly more costly to live in, who pays the differential?
- How often do you need to travel home for family reasons?
- What kind of vacation package do you require?
- What kind of support staff will you need in your new job?
- Will you need to learn a foreign language? If so, who is paying for this?
- If you have school-age children accompanying you, what kinds of schools are available, and which ones are preferred? Who pays for private school options?
- How is the quality of health care in the location? Are there back-up systems in place in case the care is inadequate in emergencies? Who pays for this?

Ask for what you require, and you may receive it. One client negotiated for an accounting firm to take on paying of household bills back home, since the partner remaining behind was not fond of this task and the employee did not want the added stress of the worry from afar. Reviewing your list will help you quantify your needs, and give you a foundation from which to negotiate and evaluate.

Some couples return home with a sense of great attachment to the people, places, and lifestyle they lived while abroad. If you are one of these families, you may want to think about long-range planning decisions together. Is there a chance to perhaps purchase housing in that country and retire there eventually, or spend part of each year there now? What about health care challenges from nation to nation and what expatriation means in terms of access to benefits? You might even decide to purchase a second residence, one you may plan to rent out part of the year, when you are back home with family. If you hope to live abroad after retirement, why not seek an expatriate posting close to that time so you can more easily move your household goods, even if you have to pay for part of the cost yourself? It will most likely be far cheaper to do it this way, unless you plan to sell off everything, store a few precious mementos, and then start over from scratch in the new location.

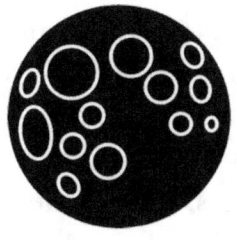

The Clash of Reunion

Many military families have reunion stories that are almost legendary in their similarity. Classic friction tales abound of newly retired couples or stories of one partner retiring or losing a job, while the other partner is still working. These are all common experiences, wrought by different circumstances in life, but speaking to people about any of these milestones can be helpful to a re-entry or reunion family. The bottom line is, when you and your spouse or partner have been separated for a significant amount of time, or your daily life patterns suddenly alter, change occurs in both of you whether or not you want to acknowledge it. Some changes are so subtle you may not even notice them until the friction of your re-entry or reunion starts rubbing you the wrong way.

For some fortunate couples used to a more calm and contented life together, simple and unexpected irritability is enough warning to stop and talk it over. They might mutually try to analyze why they are feeling the way they are and try to determine how to move forward together in a more cooperative manner. For those couples not so calm and communicative, three kinds of patterns typically emerge. In the first, both partners have noticed changes, but neither wants to talk about them. They hunker down and get through it, hiding their feelings and trying their best to maintain or reconstruct some semblance of what was normal before the separation. What if they can't restore "normal" to their relationship on their own or they are no longer compatible in some ways? In the second, one partner wants to talk it through, and the other would really rather ignore all those uncomfortable discussions and just push on, wishing the "touchy-feely" partner would leave it alone. In this case, each partner feels misunderstood and frustrated, and there is a danger of shutting down on each other. In the third, life gets out of control the fastest because both partners are expressive and hit each other between the eyes with their temper, self-righteousness, and impatience. It's hard to take back something said in the heat of anger. Without rules of engagement, chaos may erupt. But all are trying to function as best they can.

Now add children to the mix. When children are involved in a reunion, the clashes that come are fairly obvious and often out in the open, no matter how discreet parents may think they are. To the children's dismay or glee (depending upon how they react to the discord), much can be made of the dissonance between parents at these times. Age is often a factor in that perception. Older, more independent children might, on some level, feel badly their parents are fighting, but a resourceful teen will find a way to obtain a privilege, head off to a party, or otherwise push for the outrageous simply because it's a perfect opportunity to manipulate outcomes before angry, distracted parents wise up. If you are too busy arguing with your spouse or partner to see it, some kids will get away with as much as they can, while others will run to their room, slam the door, cry quietly, and hide until the latest storm blows over.

Of course, with all human behavior, there is a broad spectrum of reactions and coping mechanisms. You might be surprised which of your children has the hardest time readjusting to having you home again. For some, after a few modest skirmishes, the rules settle back in place and things improve and life finds an even keel again. But what if it doesn't? Help may be needed. It's good common sense to seek an intermediary or family therapist to help you over the re-entry hump. In some situations, just talking through what's going on with others who have been there is therapy enough. Try that first if you are shy about asking a stranger for help. Many companies and military units keep track of expat movements and create social networks for emotional support and empathy. Ask around, if you are curious. You might learn some things and make a few new friends in the process.

Military families tell stories about reunions with family members who have been deployed for months or years at a time and how the family structure can fall apart if a few ground rules aren't in place before the prodigal parent returns. The parent or caretaker at home has filled your role in your absence, and the rules may have changed, since you were not there to be consulted. One can only share so much on long-distance telephone or Internet communications. Your partner or caretaker did the best he or she could without you there to share in the burden, but changes in routine, household rules, and just the rhythm of life back home will be changed, even if not at first apparent to you. So be smart. Get a briefing from your home team before opening your mouth as a parent again. Find out what transpired in your absence, ask questions in private, and don't make judgments out loud. The best advice the most seasoned military families give is, settle in slowly, listen and learn, and don't be quick about opening your mouth in front of the children. Watch your family interact, watch how decisions are being made now, and if you disagree with the changes you see, talk it over in private.

Couples who have been separated for months at a time due to a partner accepting a foreign assignment often have honeymoon-like reunions throughout a year at company expense. During these potentially romantic R&Rs, many of which might take place in a location away from home, such as a central meeting point for travel and touring together, little is addressed in the way of how life has changed for either of you. You are so happy to be together that more serious topics do not surface. It is not until you are both together again in your home that the friction may become evident. Everything from changed levels of independence, sleep patterns, newly acquired hobbies, or even what is watched on television, to work-out habits, food choices, and mealtimes can strike you as different. If you have been connecting regularly to talk during your separation, it is relatively easy to notice these changes and talk them over together. If, however, your assignment abroad did not allow for frequent emotional contact and discourse, you might want to carve out some extra time to become reacquainted, maybe even build some new routines together.

If you wish to move forward together, you will talk about what is to come, about the hopes and dreams that may have changed for one or both of you. Looking forward at your life together, much like racing down a long runway and looking as far ahead as possible to stay on course, is a great goal. Happy landings!

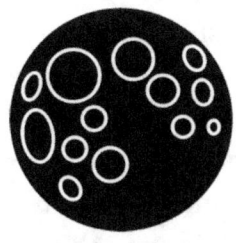

Retention & Reinvention

What organization doesn't contend with finding and keeping great people? Whether you are dealing with a club, religious community, workplace, or any type of organized setting, leaders are always challenged to find ways to attract and retain the best and brightest. Competition is fierce in the working and volunteer world, and most people are not aware of their own self-worth, especially if they have been employed at one company or task for any great length of time. Rest assured, the head-hunters of the world are noticing you, and, at the smallest scent of dissatisfaction with your present job, they will pounce. But do you really want to leave? There may be room for change. How big a change is up to you.

An employer who is not debriefing you about your time abroad is losing money. They are also losing your confidence, experience, your enthusiasm, and your

155

continuing commitment to the organization. The critical skills you have acquired may be going to waste, the lessons learned not shared with others who might also push the company forward to greater successes. The loss in this knowledge economy can be incalculable.

Smart employers will at least try to elicit some type of feedback from you, but it is usually up to you to facilitate the outcomes and delineate the applications of the information you've provided. Not everyone has had your experience, so they may not directly connect the dots as you would as naturally as breathing. If you had been sending communications of this nature throughout your assignment abroad, subtly educating your home office about the value in your observations and actions, your return would place you in a much more advantageous position to work where you want. You would have been training people back home to see how to utilize your information and why it has value and impact on the company's bottom line. If you did do this, congratulations. You may now have your pick from several key openings at the office, since leaders are already aware of your contributions and their impact. Some companies will let several relevant departments or teams know of your pending return, and you may even be flown home for internal interviews. This opportunity to use what you've learned and maximize company profits and strategy is exciting, challenging, and a positive direction for you.

For those of you returning to the same work group, many have found it a very comfortable and easy transition. If your boss or team leadership also has expatriate experience, they know what to ask you. They also know you want to be stimulated and challenged at work and have a lot to share over time with your team. But it's not so easy for everyone. Some people return feeling out of place, no longer in sync with the people, the plans, or even the community anymore. Others have accompanied a working spouse or partner overseas, and had to give up a great job, and now are facing a new job hunt. The company may provide resources to assist a partner through this re-entry job search, since they were the cause of the condition in the first place. You may want to ask if this is a benefit at your office. Not all companies openly advertise all the services they have access to, which keeps costs down, or so they think. Sometimes, if enough expats ask the same question, a new program may be developed to respond to this need.

So is it time to look for something new? Find a place where you can apply your newly acquired skills and talents, and see what you are worth on the market these days. You might be shocked at what a competitor will pay for what's in your head and who you know. Keep in mind, though, your employer is aware of this possibility. You, therefore, may have leverage in redefining your role back at the home office. If you really like much of what you are presently associated with, why not try to reinvent your role there? It's okay to dream! Create your case.

It's time to go back over that Skills Inventory you did much earlier in this book. Take a hard look at what you wrote down. Which of the skills you listed are the ones that make you feel the best about yourself? Which elements might be most useful or bring the greatest value to your employer, and under what conditions? If you can create a powerful case, you will get attention to present it and potentially earn the opportunity to develop a new position around the new you. If you can present a logical case with a clear ability to benefit for them, most employers will be willing to explore the potential, even if only temporarily, to test-drive the program and see how it performs. What have you got to lose? The worst that happens is you are turned down. Sharp managers and program leaders will then know you are shopping around, and your résumé might begin quietly circulating internally, especially if the company is keen to keep you, and what's in your head, a part of their competitive edge.

If an employer is not so smart, or you are simply at the end of fulfilling a contract and it's time to move on, the hope is you've been making friends, cultivating relationships, building bridges, and sending signals out well in advance of making a move or accepting offers. The Skills Inventory should be a foundation for dreaming again. What would you do if you could be doing anything, if money were not an object of consideration? If you could do what you love, love what you do, *and* get paid for it, what would you choose to do with your life? On re-entry, you have the great honor of taking time to ask and answer this famous question. You have a rare chance that others would envy; you have a chance to reinvent yourself. Wise employers know this, capitalize on it, and help you return home and thrive. Otherwise you have the skills and the market value to create and define your own way forward.

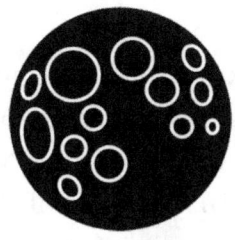

Appreciation & Application

The biggest frustration to re-entry workers is the rust they begin to feel as they come to discover they now work at a job that once suited them, but no longer fits who they are. On the surface, foreign language abilities, cross-cultural competence, and a broader, more inclusive view of the world are not being used or applied. In some cases the employer may perform some kind of re-entry assessment and try to find ways to capitalize on the new skill sets, but not all companies have the resources to accommodate these changes in personnel profiles, and not everyone is in a position to walk away from an employer for a variety of reasons. So if you can't reinvent your role and contributions at work, perhaps there are other ways to find fulfillment and make a difference. After all, don't many of us cherish a hope of making some kind of contribution to the world, however modest or great?

When you head home, whether it's to a familiar workplace and community or a new one, take time to perform an environmental scan. This is especially important if you think your job may not be as satisfying as it once was. The home you choose to live in and where it is located may help alleviate some of the fallout. Check out the socio-cultural make-up of the community. Are there cultural amenities that attract you or groups or associations of people that might interest you outside of work? Some expats find, upon re-entry, that they want to hook up with people from the country they just left behind and try to maintain linguistic and cultural ties, as well as build more friendships across the miles. Others may participate in religious or social service programs that enjoy welcoming foreign newcomers and helping them settle in, something you now know a lot about from personal experience.

You know it is not easy to accomplish what would have been the simplest of tasks back home when you are in a foreign setting. That empathy and experience can have a huge impact on new arrivals. Your employer, the one unable to accommodate the new you at work as fully as you'd hoped, might even give you time off or flex-time to offer your services in this regard. The clear satisfaction you gain by giving elsewhere has an impact on your attitude and productivity at work. Again, the smart employers figure this out and learn to work with it.

At the office, if you see knowledge deficits regarding your foreign clients or partners, you can bring great value by offering to conduct short briefings or provide insights to various work groups that have limited interaction with and knowledge of the target culture you just left behind. By putting yourself out there, you may even end up creating a new role for yourself—if the company leaders are sharp enough to see the impact of your contribution and how much it strengthens their ability to respond to foreign customers and partners. Be warned, though. Some environments are so competitive that your generous offer may not be interpreted well by others who resent your experience and your effort to create a forum to demonstrate your capabilities. If this is the case, you might be safer putting your talents to use outside the office for awhile.

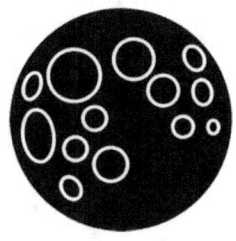

Valuing and Using
Global Leaders

Why do so many re-entry managers get restless and head off to other employers? Why are so many companies scrambling to hire managers and leaders with international experience? Why are so many young businesspeople seeking MBA degrees in international business or global management? They all have something in common. Each understands that the world is shrinking, and the most adaptable, agile companies will be globally competent, globally competitive.

Whether you are exiting military service, returning from a foreign work assignment, or returning home from studying and living abroad, the skills you have garnered can be put to immediate and powerful use. Every company should have a hiring policy that includes questions around cross-cultural competence, foreign living and language experiences, and the depth and breadth of those experiences. Even if the job for which the individual is being considered does not include responsibilities around these elements, it is wise to create a database of specific linguistic and cultural skill sets to draw upon when the time comes.

Look at what happened in the United States after the tragedies of September 11, 2001. The U.S. government suddenly noticed it had a huge deficit in its contact with talented linguists and cross-cultural experts on the regions of the world it wished to study in more depth. Calls went out to many universities and companies operating globally, calls that could have been made proactively years before, when there was no fear. Simple environmental scans, exploring the changing demographics and geopolitical concerns around the world, should have alerted us to begin broadening our own vision of what the world is and our place in it long before these events. It is an important lesson for the future: if we don't respond to global change, we will be left far behind.

Having people on staff who have a background in crossing cultures will be a given in the future. China and India, with their thriving populations and booming young economies, are going to graduate more students, create more jobs, and produce more geniuses and innovations than the rest of the world may be ready to understand or accept. And these are only two potential superpower nations, apart from the myriad other scenarios that can play out across continents and differences. Most American firms are woefully underprepared to respond to this shifting global balance of knowledge, power, and wealth. We have rested on the timeworn assumption that we are the greatest nation in the world. Think about the ethnocentrism in that notion. Doesn't everyone have pride in and love for their homeland, even if in some ways it is not perfect? How arrogant to assume we are the only ones who can feel this way about a country.

The vision and experience a global leader can bring to an organization is profound, but only if the organization is truly aware, ready for change, and willing to do some things differently in order to rise to the next level of global competence. Citizen-diplomats are valuable assets in a globally competitive setting. They can develop and advance key relationships and advise their employers, their governments, and many other agencies open to a broader, deeper world view and how it can benefit. Many of these people are around us right now, but companies and agencies have no instruments in place to capture this data or evaluate and apply it. Are you ready?

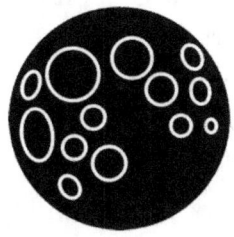

Their Growth is Your Gain

This is to the leaders out there, the employers of all kinds, in all settings around the world. If you have been wise and proactive and have been identifying and tracking the accomplishments and skills of your global workforce, you have a vast storehouse of advantages you may not be utilizing fully.

Sometimes in our race to compete, we fall short because we continue to do as we have always done. We may be uncomfortable when someone comes along in our organization who challenges the status quo and, instead of listening and considering what is being said, we become impatient, arrogant, and defensive. What are we protecting? How can we be so certain that whatever we are being told is invalid? We need to re-program ourselves to listen to even the most uncomfortable perspectives, for in doing so we may find a new approach. Returning expats have been pushing against their own comfort zones for the duration of a foreign assignment. Their own assertions have been challenged sometimes on a daily basis, and they have had to learn to lower their defensive shields and let in new ideas, new ways of looking at the world and new ways of solving problems. Just ask an expat to facilitate a meeting of global managers in your work setting and watch what happens. Instant value proposition!

Not every debriefing of a re-entry expat will be equally useful to you. Some information may simply be stored away and brought out for future review on a key word search. Some data will be so specific that you can call on it for technical consulting with a foreign client or assign a globally-savvy employee to serve on a welcome committee for a prospective customer with whom they have hobbies and cultural and linguistic experiences in common. Don't underestimate the value of bonding before business. What these sojourners have learned about how things work in other cultures and nations can save you millions of dollars and thousands of hours in human resources and contract negotiations. It sounds illogical to those of you who have never lived or worked abroad and never had to face the challenge of The Learning Curve. But to those of you who have seen deals made or broken based on trust and a true understanding and appreciation of cultural values that differ from your own, nothing more needs to be said.

If you are fortunate to already have these people in-house, then meet with them and find ways to make what's in their heads work for you. They will have many ideas and examples just waiting beneath the surface, especially if they have been feeling under-appreciated for the global skill sets they have obtained on company time and dollars. Some are burning to help, like that elementary school classmate who always groaned with excitement and raised a hand with the right answer, exploding to share it. But no one has asked. When you meet, ask a few questions, take good notes, and withhold judgment. Have the courage to think differently, to resist falling into old patterns of behavior, and to give someone little known to you a chance to create fresh new ways of approaching old challenges. You might find yourself building a new global strategies team, made up of successful expats from a variety of professions across your organization. The ones interested in participating will find you, if you get the word out.

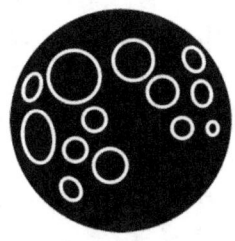

Proactive Leadership for Global Profits

Hopefully you have conducted an environmental scan of your own organization, and you have found latent global talents buried in surprising places. You might take this information and begin organizing it into useful concept clusters. Start by considering the types of functions that are needed to complete certain projects and break them down into smaller variables. Are there places where an intercultural mindset could come in handy? Absolutely.

Your sales force may have international experience, but what kind? Many sales forces have global experience without any real understanding of cultural differences and how to work across chasms in values systems. They are not learning, but may be experiencing great frustration as they try to conduct business the way we do at home. Have you made learning a foreign language mandatory and are you willing to pay for it? Do any employees who come in contact with foreign customers have at least some cultural training so they may welcome and serve each customer according to familiar values and behaviors? Your profits hinge on your ability to build, deepen, and strengthen relationships with your customers and your employees. If your company crosses cultures, so must your team's cultural competencies.

Legal teams from one culture or country to another often have no real idea of how they will achieve the corporate dictates for drawing up contracts. Of course, they know what they are doing, but they do not know how they will achieve it in a foreign setting. The concept of what a contract is can vary greatly from culture to culture. It is the relationships built that cement each contract—and allow open and frank communication as the trust grows and execution unfolds and decisions must be made or changed to move forward. Struggling with one nation's definitions while working in another is not good for business or for developing trust. Having cultural go-betweens who can advise on culturally sensitive areas around which compromise and discourse can proceed can be valuable indeed.

Don't believe this? Look at your own project timelines and budgets. Take one ongoing activity and do nothing differently. Take another one and add the interculturalist to the mix by inviting him or her to a briefing on the program. Lay out the challenges and ask for input, without any further data. Watch what happens. Let the questions come. Listen to thoughts that you would never have thought could have any possible relevance or impact. At the end of each project, compare milestones, budgets, and customer feedback. You may be surprised with the results.

Just as in real estate, we've all heard the three most important rules to buying property are "Location, location, location." It is just the same in global business endeavors, or human interaction across cultures, where the three most important rules are the three Rs: "Relationship, relationship, relationship." You probably have people in your organization who can be of immediate and cost-effective use, if only you know who they are and how to best utilize their skills.

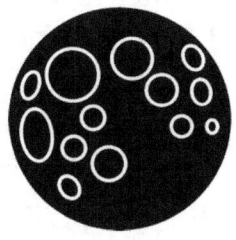

Peace, Profits, and Mutual Prosperity

As we get more comfortable in a global knowledge age, we must constantly learn and adapt to be successful. India and China, with their massive populations of over one billion people each, are going to grow exponentially, and their citizens will swarm the planet, eager to learn, develop businesses, conduct trade, and hopefully do so in an atmosphere of mutual peace and prosperity. In the nineteenth century, Britain was spanning the globe, exploring, cultivating relationships, and building an empire based on trade and intellectual advantage. Many would say the United States did much the same in the twentieth century. With the Internet and mobile telecommunications so readily available in even the most remote settings on the planet, everyone will someday have access to knowledge and economic opportunity. It is only a matter of *when.*

The playing field is equalizing. Those who do not adapt to this will weaken or perish. It makes sense that school-age children learn foreign languages and be exposed to global geography and thinking, but if the employers of a nation and those who govern that nation, do not themselves respond, learn, adapt, and create systems to absorb this changing global dynamic, how can we truly compete or collaborate in peace?

The answer lies within our people. We have global sojourners who have amassed life experiences, ways of looking at the world, and, most importantly, learned how to value and create relationships across sometimes vast cultural differences. These people may be Returning Peace Corps Volunteers (RPCVs), men and women who have served in our military or missionaries who have lived among some of the poorest people and economic conditions on our planet, and have learned that poverty is not necessarily equated with unhappiness. They may be the expatriate family just returned from two to five years abroad. Not everyone wants to capitalize on these experiences. Some will simply be glad to be home, happy they had the chance to live differently, and quietly step back into the fabric of their former lives. There are other sojourners out there, though, people whose lives and attitudes are forever altered by their experiences abroad, and they have much to offer those wise enough to ask the right questions, sit back, and listen.

Corporations have a chance to work smarter by collaborating with global service organizations and grassroots development projects in areas in which they are already present. Imagine the local service projects in developing nation communities and how cost-effectively they could be implemented with experienced leadership and deep local knowledge and trust already in place. The corporations pay the NGOs (Non-Governmental Organizations) to carry out the benevolent works and provide critical local intelligence regarding community needs and action. The United Nations would perhaps affect more rapid change by collaborating with corporate expatriates or entrepreneurs who work across borders, and the competitive and cultural intelligence and localized links to community leaders and governments would offer even more insight on how best to move forward.

Imagine global meetings of not just the elite or national leaders or corporations, but making it standard practice to include *combinations* of community leaders, corporate and governmental leaders, the military, entrepreneurs, NGOs, and academic institutions, all with a stake in the future for everyone? If we all have a seat at the table, we all can learn to build and share a common vision for a future filled with equal opportunity, access to meet basic human needs, and ways to work together to deliver the dream.

About the Author

Photo by Bao Yinghui

Linda Fraser Jacobsen is founder and president of Global Vision Strategies, LLC, an award-winning cross-cultural and global business development firm based in the United States. She holds a B.A. in English and Linguistics from Iowa State University, an M.A.T. from Georgetown University, and is presently working on her Ph.D. in International Higher Education at the University of Missouri-St. Louis. She has lived, worked, and taught around the world and believes in giving back to make a difference in as many ways as possible. She serves on numerous boards both domestic and international, among them the Sias International University Foundation in Henan, PRC, and the Atai Orphanage Fund in northern Uganda.

If you are interested in communicating, visit the Global Vision Strategies website and leave a message (www.global-visionstrategies.com). Ms. Jacobsen is a frequent keynote speaker and trainer, who often works to combine business and community service wherever she is invited. She is a member of Zonta International, an organization that holds consultative status at the United Nations and is dedicated to advancing the status of women through service and advocacy (www.zonta.org). She enjoys meeting up with sister Zontians all over the world and participating in their local service projects whenever possible.

A portion of the profits from the sale of every copy of this book will benefit:
The Atai Orphanage Fund in Uganda
www.ataiorphanage.org

The Sias International University Foundation in China
www.sias.edu.cn/en

Companies and other organizations interested in establishing global collaborations referred to by the author are especially encouraged to make contact.